经典的回声·ECHO OF CLASSICS

CW00457311

杜甫诗选
DU FU SELECTED POEMS

（新西兰）路易·艾黎　　**英译**

Translated by Rewi Alley

外文出版社
FOREIGN LANGUAGES PRESS

图书在版编目（CIP）数据

杜甫诗选/（唐）杜甫著：（新西兰）艾黎译.
一北京：外文出版社，2001．8
（经典的回声）
ISBN 7-119-02889-8

I. 杜… II.① 杜…② 艾… III. 英语－对照读物，

杜诗－汉、英 IV. H319.4:I

中国版本图书馆 CIP 数据核字（2001）第 042716 号

外文出版社网址：
　http://www.flp.com.cn
外文出版社电子信箱：
　info@flp.com.cn
　sales@flp.com.cn

经典的回声（汉英对照）
杜甫诗选

译　　者	（新西兰）路易．艾黎	
责任编辑	胡开敏	
封面设计	席恒青	
印刷监制	蒋育勤	
出版发行	外文出版社	
社　　址	北京市百万庄大街 24 号	邮政编码　100037
电　　话	（010）68320579（总编室）	
	（010）68329514／68327211（推广发行部）	
印　　刷	三河市三佳印刷装订有限公司	
经　　销	新华书店／外文书店	
开　　本	大 32 开	字　数　260 千字
印　　数	5001—8000 册	印　张　11.5
版　　次	2003 年 1 月第 1 版第 2 次印刷	
装　　别	平装	
书　　号	ISBN 7-119-02889-8 / I·695（外）	
定　　价	15.00 元	

出 版 前 言

本社专事外文图书的编辑出版,几十年来用英文翻译出版了大量的中国文学作品和文化典籍,上自先秦,下迄现当代,力求全面而准确地反映中国文学及中国文化的基本面貌和灿烂成就。这些英译图书均取自相关领域著名的、权威的作品,英译则出自国内外译界名家。每本图书的编选、翻译过程均极其审慎严肃,精雕细琢,中文作品及相应的英译版本均堪称经典。

我们意识到,这些英译精品,不单有对外译介的意义,而且对国内英文学习者、爱好者及英译工作者,也是极有价值的读本。为此,我们对这些英译精品做了认真的遴选,编排成汉英对照的形式,陆续推出,以飨读者。

外文出版社

Publisher's Note

Foreign Languages Press is dedicated to the editing, translating and publishing of books in foreign languages. Over the past several decades it has published, in English, a great number of China's classics and records as well as literary works from the Qin down to modern times, in the aim to fully display the best part of the Chinese culture and its achievements. These books in the original are famous and authoritative in their respective fields, and their English translations are masterworks produced by notable translators both at home and abroad. Each book is carefully compiled and translated with minute precision. Consequently, the English versions as well as their Chinese originals may both be rated as classics.

It is generally considered that these English translations are not only significant for introducing China to the outside world but also useful reading materials for domestic English learners and translators. For this reason, we have carefully selected some of these books, and will publish them successively in Chinese-English bilingual form.

Foreign Languages Press

目　　录
CONTENTS

杜甫诗选

DU FU SELECTED POEMS

望　岳

岱宗夫如何，齐鲁青未了。

造化钟神秀，阴阳割昏晓。

荡胸生层云，决眦入归鸟。

会当凌绝顶，一览众山小！

LOOING AT TAISHAN

Why has Taishan become so
    sacred?
See how over Qi and Lu it stands
Never losing its light blue majesty!
Endowed in the beginnings with
    such
Spirit; its sunny face and then its
    darkslopes giving
Dawn and dusk in one moment;
    cloud srising
In tiers ever refreshing it; not easy
To follow the birds as they fly
Back up its heights; one day I
    shall climb
Clear to the summit,
Seeing how small surrounding
Mountain tops appear as they lie
    belowme.

房兵曹胡马

胡马大宛名，锋棱瘦骨成。

竹批双耳峻，风入四蹄轻。

所向无空阔，真堪托死生。

骁腾有如此，万里可横行。

THE BACTRIAN HORSE

A Bactrian horse of that famous breed
Well buit for speed; with sharp ears
Standing erect, like sliced corners of
Bamboo; at the gallop four hoofs that seem
To ride on the wind; with a mount like this
Distances melt to nothing; dependable
In any emergency; its gallant spirit
Will carry one unheard-of distances
In one day's march.

画　鹰

素练风霜起，苍鹰画作殊。

㧐身思狡兔，侧目似愁胡。

绦旋光堪摘，轩楹势可呼。

何当击凡鸟，毛血洒平芜！

PAINTING OF A FALCON

Wind and frost seem to rise
From the white silk of this
Grand painting of a falcon!
The bird stares as if to pounce
On a scurrying hare, and do
I see in its eye something
Of a fierce monkey?
Chain and ring seem to invite one
To put out a hand and free it
From the perch that seems so close;
I wish I could ask it attack
Those tiny singing birds, scattering
Their blood and feathers over
The grasslands around.

奉赠韦左丞丈二十二韵

纨袴不饿死，儒冠多误身。

丈人试静听，贱子请具陈。

甫昔少年日，早充观国宾。

读书破万卷，下笔如有神。

赋料扬雄敌，诗看子建亲。

李邕求识面，王翰愿卜邻。

自谓颇挺出，立登要路津。

致君尧舜上，再使风俗淳。

TO MINISTER WEI JI

Lads who wear silk pants
Rarely starve; but now
To be dressed like a scholar
Invites destitution;

I would be grateful, sir,
If you would listen as I
Place my story before you;

In my youth I came to Chang'an,
Studied hard, read widely;
My pen seemed inspired;
People thought my prose and poetry
Compared well with the best;
Famous scholars sought my friendship;

Then began my feeling that
I was on the highway to advance,
Soon to gain recognition, thus
Assisting our Emperor to rule,
To purify, to cleanse;

此意竟萧条，行歌非隐沦。

骑驴十三载，旅食京华春。

朝扣富儿门，暮随肥马尘。

残杯与冷炙，到处潜悲辛。

主上顷见征，欻然欲求伸。

青冥却垂翅，蹭蹬无纵鳞。

甚愧丈人厚，甚知丈人真。

每于百僚上，猥诵佳句新。

窃效贡公喜，难甘原宪贫。

焉能心怏怏，只是走踆踆。

Time passed
And I became disillusioned,
Though never with the idea
That my songs should cut me off
From my world; I have been around
On a donkey these thirteen years,
And now in spring in the capital,
Each morning standing humbly
At the doors of the rich
Each evening stumping along
In the dust raised by fat horses,
Hiding bitterness when eating
Cold leftover from feast tables;

Then when recently the court
Issued invitation for good men
To work, I for one brief moment
Had hope;
Now am I still as a bird
Denied the heavens wherein to fly
Or as a fish in water
Unable to swim;

You are kind to me though
I hardly deserve it, I know too,
You have quoted my poems
To your friends, and am pleased
At your new appointment, while still
Hating my own wretchedness;
I am footsore and tired, so hope

今欲东入海，即将西去秦。

尚怜终南山，回首清渭滨。

常拟报一饭，况怀辞大臣。

白鸥没浩荡，万里谁能驯！

I am not disappointed; it is
That I simply must leave,
Go east and be beside the sea,
Which means I shall go from the capital,
Though I so love to look
At the southern mountains,
And shall miss the clear Wei River;

A hungry man will remember
The kindness in even simple food
When given him, so I will not
Forget your great thoughtfulness;
    but when
A bird vanishes through the heavens,
Who will be able to cage him again?

前出塞九首

（一）

戚戚去故里，悠悠赴交河。

公家有程期，亡命婴祸罗。

君已富土境，开边一何多！

弃绝父母恩，吞声行负戈。

（二）

出门日已远，不受徒旅欺。

骨肉恩岂断，男儿死无时！

走马脱辔头，手中挑青丝。

BEYOND THE FRONTIER

(Nine Poems)

(1)

Full of bitterness, taken
From our homes to be sent past
Far western frontiers, knowing well
That with time limits set, all
Infringements will be punished;
Wondering why the Emperor who
Controls so vast a territory
Should want to extend it; cut off
From the love of home folk,
We hold back tears, and shouldering
Spears, are forced to march away.

(2)

Long since I left home, so
No more a raw recruit;
The warmth of family love
Still remains with me, though
I know that at any moment
I might die; bridle falling off,
Reins still in my hand,

15

捷下万仞冈，俯身试搴旗。

（三）

磨刀鸣咽水，水赤刃伤手。

欲轻肠断声，心绪乱已久。

丈夫誓许国，愤惋复何有？

功名图麒麟，战骨当速朽。

（四）

送徒既有长，远戍亦有身。

生死向前去，不劳吏怒瞋。

路逢相识人，附书与六亲。

哀哉两决绝，不复同苦辛！

Or when leaping down a hillside
To seize the enemy flag below.

(3)

Grinding weapons in the gurgling stream,
A sound comes through
The swishing water as it
Suddenly turns red from hands
Cut by the blade; the sharp pain
Joining up with my bitterness;
Yet we are picked men who have
Promised to serve the Emperor,
So why should one complain? We
Shall do much, gain fame, even
Though bones left on the battlefield
Quickly change to dust again.

(4)

You are in charge of conscription
And I must go to distant frontiers,
That is that; so shall I march on,
Live or die! Needless for you to scowl
And bully more; perhaps too, I shall meet
Someone I know, and give him a letter
To bring back; sad that I must leave
My home folk without even the hope
Of sharing our hardships together.

（五）

迢迢万里余，领我赴三军。

军中异苦乐，主将宁尽闻？

隔河见胡骑，倏忽数百群。

我始为奴仆，几时树功勋！

（六）

挽弓当挽强，用箭当用长。

射人先射马，擒贼先擒王。

杀人亦有限，立国自有疆。

苟能制侵陵，岂在多杀伤？

(5)

Away into the distance
They march us to join
Frontier armies, where
For some it is easier
Than for others; how can
A commander know all?
At one river we suddenly
See the tribesmen in
Their many units; so far
I have been thought little of;
When can I show how bravely
I fight for our land?

(6)

In picking bows
We prefer taut ones;
In choosing arrows we take
The longest; in killing
The enemy we go first
For their horses; in taking
Prisoners we first capture
Commanders; yet there comes
To be a limit to killing;
A country must have boundaries
And hold them; useless to slaughter
Many people to make a victory.

（七）

驱马天雨雪，军行入高山。

径危抱寒石，指落层冰间。

已去汉月远，何时筑城还？

浮云暮南征，可望不可攀！

（八）

单于寇我垒，百里风尘昏。

雄剑四五动，彼军为我奔。

虏其名王归，系颈授辕门。

潜身备行列，一胜何足论？

(7)

I urge my horse on through
The snow, as our troops enter
Mountain ravines, then leading it,
Frozen fingers hold on to rocks as we
Wind around precipices; how long
Since I left home, when shall I
Finish building this wall
And be able to return?
Evening, and clouds go south,
I would that I could grasp them
In both hands, to go along with them.

(8)

The tribesmen muster in strength,
Hurling themselves against our defences;
All around, as far as one can see,
   the wind
Is heavy with the dust of their cavalry;
But our strength is sufficient, and
   with ease
We rout them, bringing back one
Of their great leaders as prisoner,
Roped around the neck, and delivering
   him
Into the gates of our fort; but we
Are just soldiers and fighting our task —
No sense in taking one victory too
   seriously.

（九）

从军十年余，能无分寸功？

众人贵苟得，欲语羞雷同。

中原有斗争，况在狄与戎？

丈夫四方志，安可辞固穷？

(9)

A soldier for ten years or more
I have some credit; honour forbids
Me to be as others seeking privilege;
Now wars are raging on Central Plains
As well as frontier struggles against
The tribesmen; at a time like this
A soldier must think of other things
Than rank and a life of ease; with
Fighting in every quarter, how can
Its bitterness be escaped?

兵车行

车辚辚，马萧萧，行人弓箭各在腰。

爷娘妻子走相送，尘埃不见咸阳桥。

牵衣顿足拦道哭，哭声直上干云霄！

道旁过者问行人，行人但云点行频。

或从十五北防河，便至四十西营田。

去时里正与裹头，归来头白还戍边。

边庭流血成海水，武皇开边意未已！

BALLAD OF THE
WAR CHARIOTS

The jingle of war chariots,
Horses neighing, men marching,
Bows and arrows slung over hips;
Beside them stumbling, running
The mass of parents, wives and children
Clogging up the road, their rising dust
Obscuring the great bridge at Xianyang;
Stamping their feet, weeping
In utter desperation with cries
That seem to reach the clouds;

Ask a soldier: Why do you go?
Would simply bring the answer:
Today men are conscripted often;
Fifteen-year -olds sent up the Yellow River
To fight; men of forty marched away
To colonize the western frontier;
Village elders take young boys,
Do up their hair like adults
To get them off; if they return
It will be white with age, but even then
They may be sent off to the frontier again;
Frontiers on which enough blood has
    flowed

君不闻:

汉家山东二百州,千村万落生荆杞。

纵有健妇把锄犁,禾生陇亩无东西。

况复秦兵耐苦战,被驱不异犬与鸡。

长者虽有问,役夫敢申恨?

且如今年冬,未休关西卒。

县官急索租,租税从何出?!

信知生男恶,反是生女好。

生女犹得嫁比邻,生男埋没随百草。

君不见:青海头,古来白骨无人收。

新鬼烦冤旧鬼哭,天阴雨湿声啾啾!

To make a sea, yet our Emperor still
  would
Expand his authority! Have you not
  heard
How east of Huashan many counties
Are desolate with weeds and thorns?
The strongest women till the fields,
Yet crops come not as well as before;

Lads from around here are well known
For their bravery, but hate to be driven
Like dogs or chickens; only because
You kindly ask me do I dare give vent
To grievances; now for instance
With the men from the western frontier
Still not returned, the government
Demands immediate payment of taxes,
But how can we pay when so little
Has been produced?

Now, we peasants have learnt one thing:
To have a son is not so good as having
A daughter who can marry a neighbour
And still be near us, while a son
Will be taken away to die in some
Wild place, his bones joining those
That lie bleached white on the shores
Of Lake Qinghai, where voices of new
  spirits
Join with the old, heard sadly through
The murmur of falling rain.

丽人行

三月三日天气新，长安水边多丽人。

态浓意远淑且真，肌理细腻骨肉匀。

绣罗衣裳照暮春，蹙金孔雀银麒麟。

头上何所有？翠为匌叶垂鬓唇。

背后何所见？珠压腰衱稳称身。

就中云幕椒房亲，赐名大国虢与秦。

紫驼之峰出翠釜，水精之盘行素鳞。

犀箸厌饫久未下，鸾刀缕切空纷纶。

BALLAD OF THE
BEAUTIFUL LADIES

Spring festival and spring
Is truly in the air; by the winding stream at
  Chang'an
Lovely ladies walk, looking
Proudly ahead, then exchanging
Sweet and charming smiles with
Each other; faces so beautiful,
Perfect figures showing through silk
Draperies embroidered with
Golden peacocks or silver unicorns;
Their heads dressed in kingfisher
Colours, with hanging pendants of
Cut jade; on their backs little
Over-garments studded with pearls;
Amongst this galaxy the sisters
Of Yang Gui Fei, bearing great titles;
Dishes served include the purple meat
Of camel's hump, white slices of raw
Fish on crystal plates; yet these
Hardly satisfy jaded taste; all that
Has taken so much thought and work
To prepare, left hardly touched;

黄门飞鞚不动尘，御厨络绎送八珍。

箫鼓哀吟感鬼神，宾从杂遝实要津。

后来鞍马何逡巡，当轩下马入锦茵！

杨花雪落覆白蘋，青鸟飞去衔红巾。

炙手可热势绝伦，慎莫近前丞相嗔！

Palace servants ride carefully, bringing
New dishes from the imperial kitchens;
The orchestra gives such music that
Even the hearts of devils are moved;
Important guests and their retinues
Crowd in; at last comes the greatest,
Nonchalantly, on his horse; alights
In the most important spot; catkins
Have fallen so thickly as to have
Covered spring grasses, and
With sure steps he strides across them;
Overhead, a bluebird flies off with
A red kerchief it has picked up;
Prime Minister Yang is all powerful,
His slightest touch will burn;
Best to keep clear of him and his
Evil temper.

同诸公登慈恩寺塔

高标跨苍穹，烈风无时休。

自非旷士怀，登兹翻百忧。

方知象教力，足可追冥搜。

仰穿龙蛇窟，始出枝撑幽。

七星在北户，河汉声西流。

羲和鞭白日，少昊行清秋。

秦山忽破碎，泾渭不可求。

俯视但一气，焉能辨皇州？

ON CLIMBING THE BIG PAGODA
IN CHANG'AN

At the top of the pagoda one feels
To have truly entered the sky;
Wind drums incessantly; I am
Not one free of care and here my worry
   increases; and this structure,
Representing the power of Buddha,
Makes one wish to understand
And penetrate the depths of his secrets;
Looking through the dragon and snake
Openings, one marvels at their intricacy
Of construction; the seven
Stars come into view and the Milky Way;
One knows that the sun has been forced
   down,
And that it is autumn already; clouds
Obscure the mountain; the waters
Of the clear Wei and the muddy Jing
Seem to have come together; below us
Is the mist, so can one hardly realize
Down there lies our capital;

回首叫虞舜，苍梧云正愁。

惜哉瑶池饮，日晏昆仑丘。

黄鹄去不息，哀鸣何所投？

君看随阳雁，各有稻粱谋！

There is a hardly-to-be-defined air
Near the grave of the ancient Emperor
    Shun,
And one cries for his awakening; but now
By the Jade Lake, the Queen of the
    Western
Heavens disports herself with wine, as
The sun sets behind Mount Kunlun
And yellow cranes fly aimlessly,
While the wild geese stream into
The sunset, searching for life.

贫交行

翻手作云覆手雨，

纷纷轻薄何须数。

君不见管鲍贫时交，

此道今人弃如土。

FRIENDS FROM DAYS
OF POVERTY

Today there are those changeable
As clouds or rain, their number
Too great to be even counted;
Do you remember the ancients
Guan Zhong and Bao Shuya who
Despite all helped each other
In riches and poverty? Yet now
Such are looked upon as dirt!

秋雨叹三首

(一)

雨中百草秋烂死，阶下决明颜色鲜。

著叶满枝翠羽盖，开花无数黄金钱。

凉风萧萧吹汝急，恐汝后时难独立。

堂上书生空白头，临风三嗅馨香泣。

(二)

阑风伏雨秋纷纷，四海八荒同一云。

38

MELANCHOLY IN THE
AUTUMN RAIN

(Three Poems)

(1)

A utumn rains and the vegetation
Begins to wither and die; only
Below the steps some flowers still
Stand fresh and lovely, stalks
Still bright with leaves, blooms
Shining like golden coins; but
Now as the cold wind rises so
Will they feel bitterness, and as
The days go on, they too will pass;
Now I, sitting in the room above
Writing and letting my hair grow
White ineffectively, look down
On you through my melancholy,
Breathing in your fragrance.

(2)

Wild winds and the sound of
Continuous rain; it seems
The whole universe has come
Together in one vast cloud

去马来牛不复辨，浊泾清渭何当分？

禾头生耳黍穗黑，农夫田父无消息。

城中斗米换衾裯，相许宁论两相值？

（三）

长安布衣谁比数，反锁衡门守环堵。

老夫不出长蓬蒿，稚子无忧走风雨。

雨声飕飕催早寒，胡雁翅湿高飞难。

秋来未曾见白日，泥污后土何时干？

So darkening the land that
A horse going and an ox coming
Cannot be distinguished
Which way they go;
The muddy Jing and the clear Wei
Both seem the same today! Now
Grain awaiting harvest will sprout,
Millet in head go smutty,
So that for our farming families
No hope remains;
I heard that in the city a measure
Of grain is being exchanged for bedding
Quilts, with buyers thinking
The bargain good.

(3)

Are there in this Chang'an
Other poor scholars like me
Who behind closed doors and
Within empty homes stay,
While outside wild weeds grow,
Boys splashing and wading
In the wind and rain,
A rain that already begins
To ride on the cold north wind,
Making the wings of wild geese
Too sodden for easy flight; this
Autumn we have not seen the sun,
Just being faced with dirty mud!
When, oh when, will mother earth
Become dry once again?

41

后出塞五首

（一）

男儿生世间，及壮当封侯。

战伐有功业，焉能守旧丘？

召募赴蓟门，军动不可留。

千金装马鞭，百金装刀头。

闾里送我行，亲戚拥道周。

斑白居上列，酒酣进庶羞。

少年别有赠：含笑看吴钩。

FRONTIER STORIES

(Five Poems)

(1)

Just to be a man is nothing much,
But to be made an army officer,
That surely is something!
Honour and fame come from success
In war, it seems; then why stay
In so simple a country place?

So reasoned I when called to serve
On the northern frontier; restless
As I saw others go; some spending
A thousand pieces of gold on riding
Equipment, a hundred for a sword;

When at last I went, all the village
Turned out in farewell; friends
And relatives surrounded me following
That farewell dinner where the elders
Sat in their seats of honour, plying me
With food and wine; as I went
Friends gave me a sword of famous
Make, I smiling happily as I stared
Lovingly at it.

(二)

朝进东门营，暮上河阳桥。

落日照大旗，马鸣风萧萧。

平沙列万幕，部伍各见招。

中天悬明月，令严夜寂寥。

悲笳数声动，壮士惨不骄。

借问大将谁，恐是霍嫖姚。

(三)

古人重守边，今人重高勋。

岂知英雄主，出师亘长云。

六合已一家，四夷且孤军。

遂使貔虎士，奋身勇所闻。

(2)

Dawn and we report at East Gate
Barracks, then towards evening march
Over the Heyang Bridge, our standards
Red with the glow of sunset,
Wind whistling, horses neighing;
We camp for the night on level sandy
    ground;
Units gather in appointed places
Under the bright moonlight, and then
Comes the strict order for silence
Following the clear note
Of a bugle, and we feel a little
Strange, homesick; "Who
    commands us?"
One asks; another says, "He probably"
Is like the great general Huo Piao Yao!"

(3)

Down through history have we
United to defend our borders,
Though today officials think
More of glory for themselves; then
Over all the roads our armies
Stretched out like a long cloud
And all our lands were united under
One rule, with but isolated tribesmen
Fronting us; ever our Tiger and Leopard
Troops risked all in their duty; the air

拔剑击大荒，日收胡马群；
誓开玄冥北，持以奉吾君！

(四)

献凯日继踵，两蕃静无虞。

渔阳豪侠地，击鼓吹笙竽。

云帆转辽海，粳稻来东吴。

越罗与楚练，照耀舆台躯。

主将位益崇，气骄凌上都。

边人不敢议，议者死路衢。

(五)

我本良家子，出师亦多门。

将骄益愁思，身贵不足论。

Was thick with our weapons as daily
We cut off enemy horsemen, swearing
To open up all the wild north,
Giving it as fealty to our lord.

(4)

Victories bring great processions
Of triumph, one follows the other,
And on our borders, all is quiet;
Now the gallants ride gaily to
The sound of martial music; the
Harbours are filled with ships
That come over the Eastern Sea,
Bringing silks and the produce
Of the south; now even the lower-
Ranking officers turn out
In splendid clothing; making our
Commander more full than ever
With pride and arrogance; yet no man
On this frontier would dare criticize,
For he who would do so would most
  certainly
Be found dead by the wayside.

(5)

I came from a good home, serving
The country in many place; but
The arrogant ambition of our
Commander became impossible for me;
Offers of promotion are nothing, for

跃马二十年，恐辜明主恩。

坐见幽州骑，长驱河洛昏。

中夜间道归，故里但空村。

恶名幸脱免，穷老无儿孙。

Having ridden these twenty years
I fear I no longer deserve imperial favour,
Then seeing the havoc eastern horsemen
  wreak
On our Central Plains; in the middle
Of one night and by a lonely track
I returned to my now deserted village;
A desolate welcome, but no man
Can say I have been a traitor; yet
Now here am I, poor and old, with
Neither son nor grandson to comfort me.

自京赴奉先县咏怀五百字

杜陵有布衣，老大意转拙。

许身一何愚，窃比稷与契！

居然成濩落，白首甘契阔。

盖棺事则已，此志常觊豁。

穷年忧黎元，叹息肠内热。

取笑同学翁，浩歌弥激烈。

非无江海志，萧洒送日月。

生逢尧舜君，不忍便永诀。

SONG OF THE ROAD — GOING FROMTHE CAPITAL TO FENGXIAN

I, a man from Duling, wearing only
Common hemp clothes; despite advancing
  years
And becoming ever more impractical,
Still thinking of helping the court,
Daring to imitate the ministers of old
In giving advice; surprised when
Some swift current sweeps me off my
Balance; still do I go on, even
Finding the struggle sweet; determined
To work to the end of my days, searching
For the better way; writing poems of passion
In grief for the people, burnt
Up with the agony of it all, though
My old scholar friends smile in sarcasm
When I sing of injustice;

It would be easy to follow my longing,
Leave all this, live the pure life sailing
On rivers, watching the rising
Of suns and moons; yet I believe
The Emperor can be like the best

当今廊庙具，构厦岂云缺？

葵藿倾太阳，物性固莫夺。

顾惟蝼蚁辈，但自求其穴。

胡为慕大鲸，辄拟偃溟渤？

以兹误生理，独耻事干谒。

兀兀遂至今，忍为尘埃没？

终愧巢与由，未能易其节。

沉饮聊自遣，放歌破愁绝。

岁暮百草零，疾风高冈裂。

天衢阴峥嵘，客子中夜发。

霜严衣带断，指直不得结。

Of the ancients, that he lacks not
Able men for his service; sunflowers
Reach out towards the light, which all
Living things need; one must not imitate
The ant, which seeks security in its own
    hole!

Yet why should I ever be like
That whale which always tried
To hold back the dark, oncoming sea?
These lessons have taught me much,
But I am ashamed to ever seek favours,
So do I suffer down to this day,
Still hating my obscurity;
Despite this I go on trying, never
Thinking it right to be like a hermit
Seeking only his own salvation;
Rather would I drink some wine
And sing until my sorrow passes.

Autumn brings a
Withering of the grasses that have
Grown so well; furious gales rip
Over the tall mountains; then, on
That midnight when I set out, the sky
Was like some ethereal, mysterious
Archway over me; the belt around
My garment broke, and in the frost
My fingers were too numb to tie it
Again; in the sharpest cold, just
Before sunrise, I passed by the Li
Mountain, knowing that there, above

凌晨过骊山，御榻在嵽嵲。

蚩尤塞寒空，蹴踏崖谷滑。

瑶池气郁律，羽林相摩戛。

君臣留欢娱，乐动殷胶葛。

赐浴皆长缨，与宴非短褐。

彤庭所分帛，本自寒女出。

鞭挞其夫家，聚敛贡城阙！

圣人筐篚恩，实欲邦国活。

臣如忽至理，君岂弃此物？

多士盈朝廷，仁者宜战栗！

况闻内金盘，尽在卫霍室。

Me by the pools of Huaqing Palace,
The Emperor slept; how in this dawn
In the cold mountains, by steep cliffs
And in deep valleys, soldiers tramped
On guard wearing rocks smooth; steam
Rose from the jade green pools; and there
Stood the spears and colours of the
Imperial guard, massed together; here
The court plays daily in sensuous
Pleasure; drums beat, bells ring; the
Prettily dressed may go to bathe in
The hot springs, though none in short
Clothes may join in the fun; the
Lovely white silk given as presents
In this gorgeous palace was made
By the half frozen fingers of some
Peasant woman, whose husband was
    beaten
With the riding whips of tax collectors
To make him give more; now, the gifts
Of the Emperor go out in baskets
Of different kinds; for surely his one
Desire is that all parts of the land
Should prosper; certainly, should any
At this court be unworthy, no presents
Would be made to them! Masses of
Offficials attend the court at dawn;
Those who love the people must be
Feeling humble in front of their
Responsibility! Palace plate of
Solid gold has somehow been collected

中堂舞神仙，烟雾蒙玉质。

暖客貂鼠裘，悲管逐清瑟。

劝客驼蹄羹，霜橙压香橘。

朱门酒肉臭，路有冻死骨。

荣枯咫尺异，惆怅难再述！

北辕就泾渭，官渡又改辙。

群冰从西下，极目高崒兀。

疑是崆峒来，恐触天柱折。

河梁幸未坼，枝撑声窸窣。

行李相攀援，川广不可越。

老妻寄异县，十口隔风雪。

In the apartments of powerful
Families; in the great hall, jade
Images of gods and fairies are
Clouded in incense; courtiers
Keep out the cold with robes of
The most precious fur, walk to
The lilt of the court orchestra,
Eating luxurious food; but while
There comes te reek of wines
And meats that rot inside the gates
Of these rich, the bones of the
Starving and cold are strewn along
The roadsides; wealth and poverty
Are held apart by so little; but I
Cannot dwell on this, and go on my
Road north over the Wei and Jing
Rivers; it is time of flood, the
Ferry shifting from its accustomed place,
Waters coming down from the west in
One great swirl, as though from
Some fabulous place, going on a
Desperate mission; yet still the
Bridges have held, though creaking
Dangerously; people help each
Other to cross, and at last I continue
Finding all the lesser streams swollen
And not easy to find a way over;

Nearing my destination, do I think
Of my wife in this far place, of

谁能久不顾，庶往共饥渴！

入门闻号咷，幼子饿已卒。

吾宁舍一哀，里巷亦呜咽！

所愧为人父，无食致夭折！

岂知秋禾登，贫窭有仓卒。

生常免租税，名不隶征伐。

抚迹犹酸辛，平人固骚屑。

默思失业徒，因念远戍卒。

忧端齐终南，澒洞不可掇！

Our separation by the elements, of
My own inability to support our ten
In all, of how I now come so that we
May suffer together; at long last I
Arrive, and from my home comes
The sound of crying, entering I
Learn one little one has died
Of hunger; so do I weep in my grief
And the neighbours join in mourning
With me; the shame of being father
To a child who has died of hunger
Comes home to me; how can one know
That even after harvest
The poor cannot escape more troubles?
As for me, I have never had to pay
Taxes; nor have I been liable for
Conscript service; now even a looker-on
Is sad; how much more the common man?
Then I go on to think of innocent folk,
Property seized, sons torn from their homes
  to be
Pitiful conscripts, sent off to guard
All this; and my grief rises higher
Than the Qinling Mountains; and I
Can see no end to it all.

月 夜

今夜鄜州月，闺中只独看。

遥怜小儿女，未解忆长安。

香雾云鬟湿，清辉玉臂寒。

何时倚虚幌，双照泪痕干？

MOONLIGHT NIGHT

This night at Fuzhow there will be
Moonlight, and there she will be
Gazing into it, with the children
Already gone to sleep, not even in
Their dreams and innocence thinking
Of their father at Chang'an;
Her black hair must be wet with the dew
Of this autumn night, and her white
Jade arms, chilly with the cold; when,
Oh when, shall we be together again
Standing side by side at the window,
Looking at the moonlight with dried eyes.

哀王孙

长安城头头白乌，夜飞延秋门上呼。

又向人家啄大屋，屋底达官走避胡。

金鞭断折九马死，骨肉不得同驰驱。

腰下宝玦青珊瑚，可怜王孙泣路隅。

问之不肯道姓名，但道困苦乞为奴。

已经百日窜荆棘，身上无有完肌肤。

高帝子孙尽龙准，龙种自与常人殊。

IN SORROW FOR
THE LOST PRINCE

A crow with a white head came,
They say, from the city wall and
Warned those in the great palaces
By pecking on the tiled roofs;
And the court, seeing it as a sign,
Fled, breaking their golden whips,
Killing nine of their best horses
In their mad flight; so was the
Imperial family separated;

Now, out on a country road, a youth
Of that family halts me; his
Valuables are hidden in his rags,
He sobs bitterly, refusing to give
His name; asking to be taken as a
Slave, because for over three months
Has he been hiding out in the
Waste lands, so that now his skin
Is badly torn and broken; yet still
The prominent nose of the imperial
House marks him as being different
From local lads;

豺狼在邑龙在野，王孙善保千金躯。

不敢长语临交衢，且为王孙立斯须。

昨夜东风吹血腥，东来橐驼满旧都。

朔方健儿好身手，昔何勇锐今何愚！

窃闻天子已传位，圣德北服南单于。

花门勠面请雪耻，慎勿出口他人狙。

哀哉王孙慎勿疏，五陵佳气无时无。

Swiftly did I say to him,
"Now that
Wild beasts in the shape of men
Have occupied Chang'an,
Care for your own safety,
I cannot talk with you for long
In so public a place, but you must know
There has come defeat; the east wind stank
With blood,
Rebel camel trains from
The west
Have come to the capital,
Our once fine troops were
Beaten, why has their bravery
Changed to cowardice;
The Emperor has abdicated
In favour of the prince who has
Brought in allies from Turkestan, and
These have tattooed their faces to say
They will restore the country;
Be ever vigilant of spies;
The spirits of your ancestors
Are with you, while there
Is life there is hope. "

悲陈陶

孟冬十郡良家子，血作陈陶泽中水。

野旷天清无战声，四万义军同日死。

群胡归来血洗箭，仍唱胡歌饮都市。

都人回面向北啼，日夜更望官军至。

LAMENT ON THE BATTLE
OF CHENTAO

The best of our youth
From ten districts have poured
Their blood into the bogs of
Chentao, mixing it with the mud
Of early winter; now the whole
Drear place is deserted, with
Skies clear and no sound of struggle;
Yet here some forty thousand
Of our men gave their lives, all
On one day; while now the tribesmen
Enemy wash the blood from their weapons,
Drunkenly shouting songs
In the market-places, and the people
Of Chang'an turn their faces
Stained with tears to the north,
Ever hoping for the loyal troops
To return.

对 雪

战哭多新鬼，愁吟独老翁。

乱云低薄暮，急雪舞回风。

瓢弃樽无绿，炉存火似红。

数州消息断，愁坐正书空。

SNOW

Over the battlefields
There are many new ghosts
Who weep; and I, an old man,
Sit alone, bitterly looking
Out on the wild clouds
That dull the sky, and
At the snowflakes that dance
In the whirling wind;
The gourd ladle lies beside
An empty wine pot; I can
But imagine that the stove
Gives heat; no news from
Many districts; I sit in
Desperation; really, this
Is all too impossible!

春　望

国破山河在，城春草木深。

感时花溅泪，恨别鸟惊心。

烽火连三月，家书抵万金。

白头搔更短，浑欲不胜簪。

SPRING-THE LONG VIEW

Even though a state is crushed
Its hills and streams remain;
Now inside the walls of Chang'an
Grasses rise high among unpruned trees;
Seeing flowers come, a flood
Of sadness overwhelms me; cut off
As I am, songs of birds stir
My heart; third month and still
Beacon fires flare as they did
Last year; to get news
From home would be worth a full
Thousand pieces of gold;
Trying to knot up my hair
I find it grey, too thin
For my pin to hold it together.

忆幼子

骥子春犹隔，莺歌暖正繁。

别离惊节换，聪慧与谁论。

涧水空山道，柴门老树村。

忆渠愁只睡，炙背俯晴轩。

THINKING OF MY BOY

Comes spring once more,
Pony Boy, and still we
Cannot be together; I
Comfort myself hoping
You are singing with
The birds in the sunshine;
Amazed at the change of season!
Now, you have no one to
Admire you and say, "See
What a bright lad is our
Pony Boy!" I think of
The places we would enjoy
Together; in the hills,
Down by the valley streams
Under the trees outside
The gate; but best let
Myself fall asleep and
Forget, as the sun brings
Warmth to my old back.

哀江头

少陵野老吞声哭，春日潜行曲江曲。

江头宫殿锁千门，细柳新蒲为谁绿？

忆昔霓旌下南苑，苑中万物生颜色。

昭阳殿里第一人，同辇随君侍君侧。

辇前才人带弓箭，白马嚼啮黄金勒。

翻身向天仰射云，一笑正坠双飞翼。

IN SADNESS
BESIDE THE RIVER

Trying to avoid notice,
An old farmer of Shaoling
Swallows his sobs as he walks
Out on a spring day beside
The Winding River, seeing
The many palace gates fronting
The river bank barred
And deserted, then wondering
For whom now reeds and willows
Put out their glory of green.

When once the imperial standards
Came to the South Park here,
The whole place was alight with
Colour; the first lady from Zhaoyang
Palace, sitting with our lord
In his carriage; palace ladies
Riding in front carrying bows
And arrows, their white steeds
Champing on golden bits; a lass
Would aim into the clouds, bringing
Down a pair of birds in flight.

明眸皓齿今何在，血污游魂归不得！

清渭东流剑阁深，去住彼此无消息。

人生有情泪沾臆，江草江花岂终极。

黄昏胡骑尘满城，欲往城南望城北。

Bright eyes, shining teeth, where
Are they now? Wandering ghost
Cannot return; the clear Wei ever
Flows east, and the road through
Jiange is deep; the departed
And those remaining have no news
Of each other; any born with a heart
Must let tears course down his cheeks;
Only you, grasses, flowers and river
Are as careless as ever! Evening
And tribesmen riders raise dust
As they enter the city;
I return to the southern suburbs
But turn and look expectantly
Away into the north.

喜达行在所三首

(一)

西忆岐阳信，无人遂却回。

眼穿当落日，心死著寒灰。

雾树行相引，连山望忽开。

所亲惊老瘦，辛苦贼中来。

(二)

秋思胡笳夕，凄凉汉苑春。

GRATEFUL TO HAVE COME TO THE IMPERIAL COURT

(Three Poems)

(1)

Expecting a letter from
Qiyang, but none came;
Sunset and with numbed brain
I went on through mist and forest,
Then over a road that cut
Through a range of hills, until
At last I surprised old friends
By coming in front of them; I so old,
So thin, escaping from the rebels
And all those hardships.

(2)

Evening, with the sound of tribesmen's
  music,
Did make me sad, and there
Was the sadness of seeing
Palaces lying deserted and desolate;

生还今日事，间道暂时人。

司隶章初睹，南阳气已新。

喜心翻倒极，呜咽泪沾巾。

（三）

死去凭谁报，归来始自怜。

犹瞻太白雪，喜遇武功天。

影静千官里，心苏七校前。

今朝汉社稷，新数中兴年。

Yesterday I was full of uncertainty
But today I have returned alive;
Our new Emperor may be compared
With Liu Xiu of Later Han, so now
There is promise of a bright future
Which fills me with such joy, I weep.

(3)

Should I have died in captivity
Who would have told my family?
But now I have returned and can
Enjoy looking at the snow on
Taibai Mountain, and the blue sky
At Wugong again; in court
The many officials stood calmly
In their ranks; my place in front
Of military officrs; our dynasty
Has been reborn — now counting
Its years from this day on.

羌村三首

(一)

峥嵘赤云西，日脚下平地。

柴门鸟雀噪，归客千里至。

妻孥怪我在，惊定还拭泪。

世乱遭飘荡，生还偶然遂。

邻人满墙头，感叹亦歔欷。

夜阑更秉烛，相对如梦寐。

(二)

晚岁迫偷生，还家少欢趣。

娇儿不离膝，畏我复却去。

QIANG VILLAGE

(Three Poems)

(1)

From stately mountains in purple
A setting sun throws its colour out
On to plains below; magpies fuss
Around the wicket gate, and I after
The tired long miles am home again;
Wife and children, wide eyed with surprise,
Greet me, then quickly wipe away their
    tears;
War has taken me to many places,
Never was it thought I would return; so
Neighbours get over the garden wall,
Every one sobbing out welcome; then
As darkness falls and by candle light
We stare into each other's face
As if in a dream.

(2)

I feel it a little humiliating to be
Gaining this joy at my time of life
Though in reality there is little
To be happy over; my much loved son
Stays close to me, fearing I will

忆昔好追凉，故绕池边树。

萧萧北风劲，抚事煎百虑。

赖知禾黍收，已觉糟床注。

如今足斟酌，且用慰迟暮。

（三）

群鸡正乱叫，客至鸡斗争。

驱鸡上树木，始闻叩柴荆。

父老四五人，问我久远行。

手中各有携，倾榼浊复清。

苦辞酒味薄，黍地无人耕。

兵革既未息，儿童尽东征。

请为父老歌，艰难愧深情。

歌罢仰天叹，四座泪纵横。

Go away once more; last year he and I
Explored in the trees around the pond,
But now the north wind tells of
The coming winter; I worry endlessly
About our difficulties, though grateful
Harvests have been good, and I shall
Have wine enough to solace me through
All unhappy thoughts that rise.

(3)

Such a noise from our flock of chickens
That I chase them off under the trees
To stop their fighting, for neighbours
Are here, already knocking at the garden
    gate;
They are the village elders, each with
A present for me, and into our jars
We pour their wine, the strong and the
    weak
Together, they asking pardon for
Its poorness, saying that now they have
No lads at home to plough millet fields,
For with wars continuing, their boys
Have all gone to the eastern front; then
I sing a song for them, telling them how
Sweet a thing is the sympathy of those
Who too suffer hardship, and we look
Into each other's eyes, seeing all are
Wet with tears.

北　征

皇帝二载秋，闰八月初吉。

杜子将北征，苍茫问家室。

维时遭艰虞，朝野少暇日。

顾惭恩私被，诏许归蓬荜。

拜辞诣阙下，怵惕久未出。

虽乏谏诤姿，恐君有遗失。

君诚中兴主，经纬固密勿。

东胡反未已，臣甫愤所切。

挥涕恋行在，道途犹恍惚。

乾坤含疮痍，忧虞何时毕？

THE ROAD NORTH

First day of the eighth month,
In the second year of this
Reign period, I prepared for
The road north, wondering if
Right to worry about my family
At such a time when all around
Was danger and distress,
With officials and people having
No time to rest; then too feeling
The consideration of the court
Was too high for me, granting
This leave; as I paid ceremonial
Farewell, at heart I feel truly
Unhappy, knowing in my work had been
Many mistakes, yet knowing still
There were things I could suggest
That would help the Emperor who,
Not long in power, ruled ably and
Planned carefully; the rebellion
Of eastern tribesmen was not yet
Subdued, and I full of anger wept
As I left the court in exile, thinking
Over the plight of our land, wondering

靡靡逾阡陌，人烟眇萧瑟。

所遇多被伤，呻吟更流血。

回首凤翔县，旌旗晚明灭。

前登寒山重，屡得饮马窟。

邠郊入地底，泾水中荡潏。

猛虎立我前，苍崖吼时裂。

菊垂今秋花，石戴古车辙。

青云动高兴，幽事亦可悦。

山果多琐细，罗生杂橡栗。

或红如丹砂，或黑如点漆。

雨露之所濡，甘苦齐结实。

缅思桃源内，益叹身世拙。

坡陀望鄜畤，岩谷互出没。

我行已水滨，我仆犹木末。

When all our worry and sadness would
    cease;
Paths wound across the countryside,
Smoke from kitchens rare to see;
I met many wounded, who groaned
As they bled; looked back towards
Fengxiang until banners disappeared
In the fading light, then turned into
The tumbled, freezing hills, halting
At times to water my horse, coming
To flat country around Binzhou
Cut through by the Jing River's flow;
Then to a mass of jumbled rocks
Standing out like tigers;
I saw wild chrysanthemums fading,
And noted the marks of ancient carts
Over rocks; as I rode higher
So did my spirits rise, pleased with
The clouds in the blue sky and all
The quietness, finding tiny wild berries
Amongst acorns and chestnuts,
Some red as cinnabar, others black
As lacquer, watered by the rain and dew;
Some sweet, some bitter, and I thought
How good it was to be close to nature;
Then wondered if, after all, I had lived
Rightly or not;

Rising from a path I looked at last
Over the plateau of Fuzhou; gullies,
Precipices came and went, and I was down

鸱鸮鸣黄桑，野鼠拱乱穴。

夜深经战场，寒月照白骨。

潼关百万师，往者散何卒？

遂令半秦民，残害为异物。

况我堕胡尘，及归尽华发。

经年至茅屋，妻子衣百结。

恸器松声回，悲泉共幽咽。

平生所娇儿，颜色白胜雪。

见爷背面啼，垢腻脚不袜。

床前两小女，补绽才过膝。

海图坼波涛，旧绣移曲折。

天吴及紫凤，颠倒在短褐。

老夫情怀恶，呕泄卧数日。

那无囊中帛，救汝寒凛栗。

By the river while my serving lad
Still remained among the trees above;
Owls hooted from withered mulberry leaves,
Field mice scampered from hole to hole;
Then in the night we passed an old attlefield,
The cold moonlight shining on bleached bones,
And I thought of the end of the vast army
Defeated at Tongguan, wondering why
People this side of the Yellow River
Should have been butchered too;

I have suffered from the tribesmen
So that my hair has turned white;
A whole year since last I came home,
Now finding my wife in patched clothes;
Her crying on greeting me like the sound
Of wind through the pines, our tears
Falling like water from a spring; Pony Boy
I have ever loved so well, with a face
As white as snow, turning away to weep,
And I seeing his dirty bare feet;
The two girl children in scanty patched
Clothes not reaching their knees, little skirts
Cut down from old robes so that the
    embroidery
Was a confused picture of monsters
And phoenixes; and I growing old
Am sick at heart, staying in bed
A day or two to regain my strength,
Feeling it fortunate that I brought
Along some cloth to help the family
Against winter's cold; cosmetics too

粉黛亦解包，衾裯稍罗列。

瘦妻面复光，痴女头白栉。

学母无不为，晓妆随手抹。

移时施朱铅，狼藉画眉阔。

生还对童稚，似欲忘饥渴。

问事竞挽须，谁能即嗔喝。

翻思在贼愁，甘受杂乱聒。

新归且慰意，生理焉得说。

至尊尚蒙尘，几日休练卒？

仰观天色改，坐觉妖氛豁。

阴风西北来，惨淡随回纥。

其王愿助顺，其俗善驰突。

They find in my baggage and some bedding
Quilts, so that my wife is happy again
And the silly children try to do up
Their hair, copying their mother; sticking
Fingers into the morning make-up,
Plastering rouge and powder
On their cheeks, making eyebrows
That look really silly; soon
I begin to be glad I am alive,
And can be with them all, forgetting
The hunger and thirst of the past;

They ply me with questions, children
Pulling my beard in fun; how could I be
Angry and try to stop them
After all the hard times gone through?
So I suffer all this thankfully,
For united again with my own folk I can
Rest among them for a while as we
Talk over the problem of how to gain
Livelihood for all; our Emperor
Is still in the dust of exile, and
We know not when peace will come again;
Staring into the heavens I search
For a sign, feeling that evil times
Must soon come to an end; down from
The northwest drives a cold hard wind
Urging along the Uighur riders
Now allied to our rightful cause;
Their men are tough horsemen,

送兵五千人，驱马一万匹。

此辈少为贵，四方服勇决。

所用皆鹰腾，破敌过箭疾。

圣心颇虚伫，时议气欲夺。

伊洛指掌收，西京不足拔。

官军请深入，蓄锐可俱发。

此举开青徐，旋瞻略恒碣。

昊天积霜露，正气有肃杀。

祸转亡胡岁，势成擒胡月。

胡命其能久，皇纲未宜绝。

忆昨狼狈初，事与古先别。

奸臣竟菹醢，同恶随荡析。

不闻夏殷衰，中自诛褒妲。

They come, five thousand cavalry
With ten thousand horses;
Their policy to use a small force,
Their courage apparent to all; they
Are best used as hunting falcons,
So that the enemy front
May be pierced as with
An arrow; the Emperor thinks them good,
Yet councillors are unhappy
With this decision;

Now Loyang can be retaken, and after that
Chang'an will be ours again; best for
Imperial armies to march east, gain
Their positions, then attack, getting
Into Shandong, then driving northeast;
Autumn changes to winter, the time for
Cold hard justice which needs to kill;
Rebels unable to last long; our dynasty
Will continue; and I think back
To the beginning of the rebellion,
How we had left tradition, and had
The worst minister executed, his useless
Friends sent away; Xia and Yin ended
But their leaders did not execute
The women who had caused the evil;
We will compare our Emperor
With those who were halted, and then
Marched on again, like leaders who brought

周汉获再兴，宣光果明哲。

桓桓陈将军，仗钺奋忠烈。

微尔人尽非，于今国犹活。

凄凉大同殿，寂寞白兽闼。

都人望翠华，佳气向金阙。

园陵固有神，洒扫数不缺。

煌煌太宗业，树立甚宏达。

The courts of Zhou and Han to life
Once more; we are grateful to Chen Xuanli,
The brave and loyal hero, who led
So well, for without him we might have
    lost;
Now because his victories come,
Our dynasty takes power again;

Datong Hall where once the court
Gathered for audience is empty;
None comes to Baishou Gate where before
Councillors met; anxiously Chang'an folk
    await
The great return and a new, more
Brilliant period; the spirits of
Imperial ancestors are still around us;
Rites due to them will be carried through
As ever; the empire that Tai Zong built
Is set on solid foundations again.

彭衙行

忆昔避贼初，北走经险艰。

夜深彭衙道，月照白水山。

尽室久徒步，逢人多厚颜。

参差谷鸟鸣，不见游子还。

痴女饥咬我，啼畏虎狼闻。

怀中掩其口，反侧声愈嗔。

小儿强解事，故索苦李餐。

一旬半雷雨，泥泞相牵攀。

THE ROAD TO PENGYA

How well one remembers our days
Of difficulty, danger and hardship,
Fleeing northward; night near Pengya
With a clear moon painting hill
And stream a brilliant white; on the road
Our whole family on foot
Ashamed to meet others because
Of our poor condition;
The cry of birds echoing wildly
Through valleys, passing none
Going back the way we had come;

My hungry girl child biting me
And wailing, and I fearing wild animals
Would attack, covering her mouth
To stop her noise, which but made her
Scream all the more; and then
My little lad, old enough to understand,
Searching for bitter wild berries
To eat;

For the ten days we trudged, heavy
Rains fell, so that we held on
To each other through the sticky mud

既无御雨备，径滑衣又寒。

有时经契阔，竟日数里间。

野果充餱粮，卑枝成屋椽。

早行石上水，暮宿天边烟。

小留同家洼，欲出芦子关。

故人有孙宰，高义薄层云。

延客已曛黑，张灯启重门。

暖汤濯我足，剪纸招我魂。

从此出妻孥，相视涕阑干。

众雏烂熳睡，唤起沾盘飧。

誓将与夫子，永结为弟昆。

With nothing to keep off the rain,
Shivering as we went over slippery paths
In suffering and bitterness, at times
Walking all day, though really covering
But a few miles; living off the land,
Sleeping under trees; each day
When we set out, all was wet; sunset
As we halted, the air would be heavy
With mist;

Resting a while at Tongjiawa
We pressed on through Luzi Pass
To the home of my friend Sun,
A former magistrate, who in deep
Consideration opened his doors for us,
Lit a lamp, brought water to wash
My feet, cut paper to call back
My flagging spirit, then called
His wife and children to welcome us,
They in tender sympathy weeping as they
Heard our tale; my children could
Not hear as they had already fallen
Asleep until my friend wakened them
With food; then he felt we should
Be blood brothers, moving out his effects

遂空所坐堂，安居奉我欢。

谁肯艰难际，豁达露心肝。

别来岁月周，胡羯仍构患。

何当有翅翎，飞去坠尔前！

And giving us his room, inviting me
To live with him, saying that whatever
We wanted he would do; a friend like this
At a time of trouble could be but one
Like Sun; once we were together, then
The years parted us; tribesmen were
Fighting us then, and still do they
Give us trouble! How I would like to
Have wings and fly back to him.

曲江二首

(一)

一片花飞减却春，风飘万点正愁人。

且看欲尽花经眼，莫厌伤多酒入唇。

江上小堂巢翡翠，苑边高冢卧麒麟。

细推物理须行乐，何用浮名绊此身？

THE WINDING RIVER

(Two Poems)

(1)

Every bit of fallen blossom
Means so much less of spring;
I grieve to see petals flying
Away in the wind, yet happy
To let eyes rest on what still
Remains; drinking some wine
Though I know it is bad for me;
Kingfishers flit around
A little pavilion on the river bank;
By a tall grave-mound out on open
Ground stands a unicorn in stone;
Nature ever calls people to live
Along with her; why should I be lured
By transient rank and honours?

（二）

朝回日日典春衣，每日江头尽醉归。

酒债寻常行处有，人生七十古来稀。

穿花蛱蝶深深见，点水蜻蜓款款飞。

传语风光共流转，暂时相赏莫相违。

(2)

After andience each day, I take
Some spring clothing to pawn; evening
And I return home drunk, now having
Debts for wine all over the place;
Few men ever reach seventy, and I watch
Butterflies going deeper and deeper
In amongst the flowers, dragon-flies
Skimming and flicking over the water;
Wind, light, and time ever revolve;
Let us then enjoy life as best we can.

赠卫八处士

人生不相见，动如参与商。
今夕复何夕，共此灯烛光。
少壮能几时，鬓发各已苍！
访旧半为鬼，惊呼热中肠。
焉知二十载，重上君子堂。
昔别君未婚，儿女忽成行。
怡然敬父执，问我来何方。
问答未及已，儿女罗酒浆。
夜雨剪春韭，新炊间黄粱。
主称会面难，一举累十觞。
十觞亦不醉，感子故意长。
明日隔山岳，世事两茫茫。

WRITTEN FOR THE
SCHOLAR WEI

Our lives have been lived in different
   worlds;
Yet this night we come together,
Talking while the lamplight lasts;
Once we were young together, but the days
Have gone so fast, and now the hair on our
   temples
Has changed to white;
We speak of old friends now gone; a chance
Has brought me to you; when we parted
Twenty years ago, you had not married, now
You have a troupe of sons and daughters,
Big to small; they were so kind
To me, asking me where I came from, glad
I am their father's friend; without waiting
For more words bringing wine, going out
Into the rain to cut fresh vegetable to put
With my bowl of hot millet; and you say
How difficult it has been for us to meet,
Drinking ten toasts to me, one after another,
Yet we do not get drunk, inspired by
The warmth of your affection;
And tomorrow hills and valleys
Will separate us again, and we will each return
To our own affairs.

观　兵

北庭送壮士，貔虎数尤多。

精锐旧无敌，边隅今若何。

妖氛拥白马，元帅待雕戈。

莫守邺城下，斩鲸辽海波。

ON SEEING NEW ARMIES COME

Beiting in the northwest now
Sends in forces, with more behind –
Armed reinforcements, fierce as
Leopards or tigers; high spirited,
Never yet defeated; now, how fare
Our eastern frontiers?
Enemy leaders on white chargers
Still roam; our general awaits
His orders; I can only advise, do
Not waste energy on a siege of Ye,
Rather strike back at the enemy base
In Liao by the northeastern sea.

洗兵马

中兴诸将收山东，捷书夜报清昼同。

河广传闻一苇过，胡危命在破竹中。

只残邺城不日得，独任朔方无限功。

京师皆骑汗血马，回纥馁肉葡萄宫。

已喜皇威清海岱，常思仙仗过崆峒。

三年笛里关山月，万国兵前草木风。

ON WASHING WEAPONS

Commanders of victory recover
Our eastern lands; glad reports
Come continually; our men have
Stridden the Yellow River, and
The enemy's defeat is as simple
As axe splitting bamboo;
Yeh, their citadel, must soon
Fall to us; all this comes
From the confidence placed in
Our armies and help given them!
In our capital, officers ride
Those famous horses that sweat
Blood; our allies are feasted
In the palace; now that the
Northeast has been recaptured
And the Emperor is returning;
We rejoice, remembering
Those dark days of moving
Here and there; for so many years
Our troops have sung the songs
Of bitterness and struggle; their
United strength will clear away
The enemy, like a wind carrying

成王功大心转小，郭相谋深古来少。

司徒清鉴悬明镜，尚书气与秋天杳。

二三豪俊为时出，整顿乾坤济时了。

东走无复忆鲈鱼，南飞觉有安巢鸟。

青春复随冠冕入，紫禁正耐烟花绕。

鹤驾通宵凤辇备，鸡鸣问寝龙楼晓。

攀龙附凤势莫当，天下尽化为侯王。

汝等岂知蒙帝力，时来不得夸身强。

关中既留萧丞相，幕下复用张子房。

张公一生江海客，身长九尺须眉苍。

征起适遇风云会，扶颠始知筹策良。

Grass and leaves before it; our
Four leading generals show
Vigilance, understanding, experience,
Love of their cause; Heaven has
Given us these to save all
And to bring back security;
Now, people may go home,
Living in peace, like birds
In their nests; the spirit
Of spring is with the richly
Dressed officials at court;
Incense mixes with the scent
Of flowers; all night
The imperial carriage is prepared
For the Emperor to pay proper
Respects to his father in the morning;
At court are many, only powerful
Because they stayed with us
In exile; the whole place seems
Crowded with the titled great, though
There are many who can do little;
Useful — they should be glad of
Their good fortune, rather than
Proud of their heroism; yet good
Ministers for administration are
Chosen; for the army there is
That Zhang, nine feet tall, with
Dark eyebrows and beard; he
Comes to power at the right time
To help to save the dynasty; all

青袍白马更何有，后汉今周喜再昌。

寸地尺天皆入贡，奇祥异瑞争来送。

不知何国致白环，复道诸山得银瓮。

隐士休歌紫芝曲，词人解撰河清颂。

田家望望惜雨干，布谷处处催春种。

淇上健儿归莫懒，城南思妇愁多梦。

安得壮士挽天河，净洗甲兵长不用！

Know his advice is right; the enemy
Cannot hope for success now,
The glories of Tang will be revived;
Now every nation under the sun
Will send tribute; wonderful
Presents will come; a country now
Unknown may send some magical
White jade ring; perhaps new riches
Will be found in our hills; our
Ministers will not think of
Retirement, while all scholars will
Write in praise of peace and wise
Rule; but now, drought worries
Farmers who should be starting
Spring planting; soon our brave lads
Will return after victory to rejoin
Their families; I dream that there
Might come some great man, who
Would bring down the River of Heaven
Cleaning all the weapons of blood,
So that they could be stored away
For ever, never to be used again.

新安吏

客行新安道，喧呼闻点兵。

借问新安吏，县小更无丁？

府帖昨夜下，次选中男行。

中男绝短小，何以守王城？

肥男有母送，瘦男独伶俜。

白水暮东流，青山犹哭声！

莫自使眼枯，收汝泪纵横。

眼枯即见骨，天地终无情。

我军取相州，日夕望其平。

THE CONSCRIPTING OFFICER
AT XIN'AN

Travelling through Xin'an
I heard a bellowing voice
Taking roll call, and a local official
Told me how all grown lads
Had already gone, and now the call
Was for boys in their teens, many
Short and many thin, he wondering
How such could help to defend cities;
As I stood I saw how the fat boys
Had mothers to farewell them, but how
Lone and pitiful the thin ones were;
Evening came, and I looked at the stream
Flowing east, heard the sound
Of sobbing from among green hills
Around; and thought it were best
For those mothers not to wither
Their eyes with weeping, for even
If eyes went to skin and bone, it would
Be to no avail; now our armies were
Besieging Yecheng, and soon it should fall;

岂意贼难料，归军星散营。

就粮近故垒，练卒依旧京。

掘壕不到水，牧马役亦轻。

况乃王师顺，抚养甚分明。

送行勿泣血，仆射如父兄。

How could we have thought the rebellion
Would drive the way it did, and our army
Scatter in retreat? Now our forces
Protect granaries, train new men, dig
Fortifications that do not go down
To water, while work on tending
Cavalry mounts is not hard, and all men
Are well fed; so no need for you to weep
    more!
Guo Ziyi treats his men as his
Own children.

潼关吏

士卒何草草，筑城潼关道。

大城铁不如，小城万丈余。

借问潼关吏，修关还备胡？

要我下马行，为我指山隅。

连云列战格，飞鸟不能逾。

胡来但自守，岂复忧西都！

丈人视要处，窄狭容单车。

艰难奋长戟，万古用一夫。

哀哉桃林战，百万化为鱼。

请嘱防关将，慎勿学哥舒！

THE CONSCRIPTING OFFICER
AT TONGGUAN

The soldiers worked hard, building
Stamped earth fortifications
At Tongguan; massive walls, stronger than iron,
And smaller walls run across the high hills.
I asked an officer,
"Are these walls built
Against the tribesmen after they have routed us?"
For a reply, he asked me to dismount,
And directed my eyes to the hilltop
Where the ramparts seemed to meet the
    clouds
So that a bird might hardly pass,
And said that if we stood by the defences at Tongguan,
There was no need to worry about Chang'an;
Then he showed me how our defences
Admitted but one cart at a time,
How, when danger came, a single swordsman
Sufficed to hold the pass;
To which I made reply,
He should remember the battle of Taolin,
Where many thousands drowned in the
    Yellow River,
And tell all commanders to be vigilant
And avoid the fault of Geshu Han.

石壕吏

暮投石壕村，有吏夜捉人。

老翁逾墙走，老妇出门看。

吏呼一何怒，妇啼一何苦！

听妇前致词："三男邺城戍。

一男附书至，二男新战死。

存者且偷生，死者长已矣！

室中更无人，惟有乳下孙。

有孙母未去，出入无完裙。

老妪力虽衰，请从吏夜归。

THE CONSCRIPTING OFFICER
AT SHIHAO

Sunset and I came to Shihao Village,
Then at night stamped in an official
With pressgang; over the courtyard wall
An old man vanished, his wife going
To the door to meet demands as best
She could; in a raging temper the officer
Swore at her, she replying bitterly
So that I heard her every word:
"I have had three sons taken to be
Soldiers at Yecheng; from one
Came a letter saying his two brothers
Had been killed; he knew not
On which day he himself would die; now
In this house there lives but
A baby grandson whose mother
Still suckles him, she without
Even clothing to cover her!
I am an old woman, without much strength
But I can go with you to the battle

急应河阳役，犹得备晨炊。"

夜久语声绝，如闻泣幽咽。

天明登前途，独与老翁别。

At Heyang, there I can cook; take me,
Spare them! "
Night wore on, and the sound
Of voices died away, leaving but
The low sound of sobbing; dawn when
I rose to go, there remained only
The old man to bid me goodbye.

新婚别

兔丝附蓬麻，引蔓故不长。

嫁女与征夫，不如弃路旁。

结发为妻子，席不暖君床。

暮婚晨告别，无乃太匆忙！

君行虽不远，守边赴河阳。

妾身未分明，何以拜姑嫜？

父母养我时，日夜令我藏。

生女有所归，鸡狗亦得将。

君今往死地，沉痛迫中肠！

誓欲随君去，形势反苍黄。

LAMENT OF THE NEW WIFE

The gentle creeper cannot grow
If just clinging to flax;
To marry a soldier is worse
Than being abandoned by the road!
My hair is done up as a wife's
But we had scarcely warmed
Our bed together, when in the morning
After marriage, he rode away!
Though not so far from me, with
The front but at Heyang, still
I cannot join him as a wife, yet
Feel too bashful to go and serve
His parents; my family brought me up
But when they gave me to be a bride
They hardly thought I would be left
More miserable than a dog or hen;
Now he marches along with death
And I am full of bitterness; useless
To demand my place beside him, for
I know that would not help him; best

勿为新婚念，努力事戎行。

妇人在军中，兵气恐不扬。

自嗟贫家女，久致罗襦裳。

罗襦不复施，对君洗红妆。

仰视百鸟飞，大小必双翔。

人事多错迕，与君永相望！

He forgets me, so he might do
His duty better, leaving me
To think how I, daughter of a poor home,
Struggled hard to get the silk clothes
I now lay away; how now it is best
To wash off cosmetics, staring out
At the birds big and small who pair
So happily together, thinking how
The affairs of men are not arranged
As well as these, he and I in separation
Being simply allowed our longing
For one another.

垂老别

四郊未宁静，垂老不得安。

子孙阵亡尽，焉用身独完？

投杖出门去，同行为辛酸。

幸有牙齿存，所悲骨髓干。

男儿既介胄，长揖别上官。

老妻卧路啼，岁暮衣裳单。

孰知是死别，且复伤其寒！

此去必不归，还闻劝加餐！

土门壁甚坚，杏园度亦难。

THE OLD COUPLE PART

War everywhere, and though old
I cannot have peace, for with
Sons and grandsons killed, life
For me has little meaning;
So now throwing away my stick
I leave home again, pitied by
My comrades, yet telling myself
I still have some teeth, though
My bones are brittle; fitting up
As a soldier, then reporting to
An officer to take his orders;

On leaving I pass my old wife
Crying as she kneels by the path;
Notice how the winter wind blows
Through her thin clothing; think
How unlikely it is that we shall
Ever meet again, then worry that
She may catch cold, she simply
Telling me to eat well and take care;
Fortifications at Tumen Pass are strong,
River crossings at Xingyuan difficult;

势异邺城下，纵死时犹宽。

人生有离合，岂择盛衰端？

忆昔少壮日，迟回竟长叹。

万国尽征戍，烽火被冈峦。

积尸草木腥，流血川原丹。

何乡为乐土，安敢尚盘桓！

弃绝蓬室居，塌然摧肺肝。

Yet there the situation is better than at
Yecheng; maybe there is still some time
To live, though one knows that separation
From life is a common enough thing,
　for both
Young and old; how I regret bygone
　days for
Now all our land is mad with war;
Beacon fires smoke, corpses
Lie stinking amongst the grass, and th blood
Of our people stains the countryside,
Making one wonder where peace and joy
May be found; things at home as bad as on
The frontier; now no reason for me to stay!
I must go, for sorrow has broken my heart.

无家别

寂寞天宝后，园庐但蒿藜！

我里百余家，世乱各东西。

存者无消息，死者为尘泥。

贱子因阵败，归来寻旧蹊。

久行见空巷，日瘦气惨凄。

但对狐与狸，竖毛怒我啼！

四邻何所有，一二老寡妻。

宿鸟恋本枝，安辞且穷栖？

方春独荷锄，日暮还灌畦。

THE HOMELESS

In the Tian Bao period, confusion reigned,
Cutting me off from my old home, leaving it
Deserted, surrounded with high weeds; more
Than a hundred families were dispersed
With no news of each other, the dead simply
Turning to dust or mud wherever they lay;
Then after defeat, I returned
Miserably, along the old familiar
Paths, walking around finding
All changed, naught but ruins under
A dull and heavy sky; a dismal place,
The only living things wild cats
And foxes, their hair standing on end
As I surprised them, so that I wept
With all the hopelessness, seeing how
The folk had gone, only a few widows
Hanging on, trying to exist, and I
Thought of how a bird will not leave
Its nest, so decided to stay on
This spring and till my land again;
Taking tools and toiling right through
The days preparing for the crop to come;

县吏知我至，召令习鼓鞞。

虽从本州役，内顾无所携。

近行止一身，远去终转迷。

家乡既荡尽，远近理亦齐！

永痛长病母，五年委沟溪。

生我不得力，终身两酸嘶。

人生无家别，何以为蒸黎？

But the local conscripting official
Heard I had returned, and sent for me
To follow the drums again, so I must march
With none to farewell, one lone lad;
Yet as there is little left to leave
It is easy to go, I caring naught whether
The road is far or near; hard times
Seem to be my lot, and I think of my
   mother
Sick five years, dying in poverty,
Bearing me, but getting little
In return; wife, mother sacrificed to war,
How can one call oneself a man
Without a home to say farewell to?

夏夜叹

永日不可暮，炎蒸毒我肠。

安得万里风，飘飖吹我裳。

昊天出华月，茂林延疏光。

仲夏苦夜短，开轩纳微凉。

虚明见纤毫，羽虫亦飞扬。

物情无巨细，自适固其常。

念彼荷戈士，穷年守边疆。

何由一洗濯，执热互相望。

A SUMMER NIGHT

With a sun that never seems to set
The heavy heat saps one's life;
How would I love
A stiff wind to rise, and
Lift my gown, playing around
My body! A sky still
And clear with the light of
The full moon throwing its beams
Over trees; in midsummer
Nights are too short; I fling
Open doors letting
Cool air come in and moonlight
Brighten empty rooms;
Everywhere insects are flying,
And I ponder on how all
Living creatrues have feelings,
All trying to do their best for
Their own well-being; so do I
Go on to think of our soldiers
Standing under arms
Guarding our frontiers; no
Way for them to bathe in cool
Waters; always vigilant, yet ever

竟夕击刁斗，喧声连万方。

青紫虽被体，不如早还乡。

北城悲笳发，鹳鹤号且翔。

况复烦促倦，激烈思时康。

Grappling with dsert heat;
Beating gongs as sentry
Duties change over through the
Nights — a sound familiar now
On all our frontiers;
Bright uniforms never compensating
For life in villages they
Have left; from northern cities
There comes sad border music;
Cranes fly overhead, calling
Each other; so here, I stop my
Worrying, just letting
My mind roam back over thoughts
Of happier days.

佳　人

绝代有佳人，幽居在空谷。

自云良家子，零落依草木。

关中昔丧乱，兄弟遭杀戮。

官高何足论，不得收骨肉。

世情恶衰歇，万事随转烛。

夫婿轻薄儿，新人美如玉。

合昏尚知时，鸳鸯不独宿。

但见新人笑，那闻旧人哭！

THE LOVELY LADY

Surely
The most lovely of her day
Now relegated to this back valley,
Memories of happier days buried
With her amidst wild greenery;

The fall of the capital has taken
Her brothers; not even did their
Great rank save them, or enable
Their corpses to be found;

The world has no time to waste
On the unlucky; love is like
A candle in the wind; her husband
Has found a new woman already, in
His eyes as beautiful as jade;

Leaves fold up together at dusk,
The wild duck does not sleep alone;
Her man sees his new favourite
Smile, but does not hear
His old one weep;

在山泉水清，出山泉水浊。

侍婢卖珠回，牵萝补茅屋。

摘花不插发，采柏动盈掬。

天寒翠袖薄，日暮倚修竹。

In the mountains the water flows
Well and clear; but down on the easy
Plains, it grows muddy; she has sent
Her maid to sell bits of jewellery for food,
Then returning, help her to pull vines
And mend the broken hut;

She picks a flower, though not
To wear in her hair; cuts a bundle
Of pine branches; there is chill
In the air and her sleeves of coloured cloth
Are thin; yet unheeding, she stands
Leaning against a bamboo,
Watching the sunset.

梦李白二首

（一）

死别已吞声，生别常恻恻！

江南瘴疠地，逐客无消息。

故人入我梦，明我长相忆。

恐非平生魂，路远不可测。

魂来枫林青，魂返关塞黑。

君今在罗网，何以有羽翼？

DREAMING OF LI BAI

(Two Poems)

(1)

When love is cleft in twain by death,
    a man
Can but try to banish his sorrow;
But when the loved one still lives on,
There remains that deep
Longing for him; now, from the miasma
Of southern waters, no news comes to me
Of you; so do you fill my dreams,
Which shows how I think of you,
Yet I worry whether this means
You are dead or alive; separated
By so great a distance, how may
I know? Then again I raeson, as you
Are held in exile, how could
You be here?

I saw you coming through
The green woods, then over
The pass on the frontier
You turned and left me;
As you are in chains,
How can you come thus on wings?

落月满屋梁，犹疑照颜色。

水深波浪阔，无使蛟龙得。

（二）

浮云终日行，游子久不至。

三夜频梦君，情亲见君意。

告归常局促，苦道来不易。

江湖多风波，舟楫恐失坠。

出门搔白首，若负平生志。

冠盖满京华，斯人独憔悴！

150

I awoke, and the last light
Of a dying moon shone over
The ceiling; I felt I could
Still see your face in the dim
Light; the waters flow deep,
And their waves rise high; I
Fear for your safety in all
The dangers that surround you.

(2)

Daily the clouds drift
Over the sky; and thinking
Of their ephemeral going and coming,
I wonder if you will ever return;
The more, because these three nights
Have I dreamed of you; and you
Seemed as real and as dear to me
As if you were beside me; then
You said you had to go, and that
To come had not been easy; the
Hard roads, the storms on lakes,
One man against the elements in
A single, tiny boat; and then as
You went, you stood up and looked
At me; rubbing your head as if
Regretting unrealized ideals;
This, the dream and now
I think of all the host of proud
Officials who throng the capital;
Knowing well you are lonely and sad;

孰云网恢恢，将老身反累。

千秋万岁名，寂寞身后事！

Who can say there is justice
Under heavean? Yet in the end
You have met this trouble;
Though when they are but forgotten dust,
Your name for a thousand years, and then
Ten thousand more, will stand with men;
Yet I grieve
That such will be small comfort to you
When you have passed.

秦州杂诗二十首(选二)

(一)

满目悲生事，因人作远游。

迟回度陇怯，浩荡及关愁。

水落鱼龙夜，山空鸟鼠秋。

西征问烽火，心折此淹留。

QINZHOU

(Two of Twenty Poems)

(1)

Troubles fill our lives;
It is man who has made me
Take these hard roads; slowly
We wind up Long Mountain,
Scared to look down the cliffs
In the pass we go through;
At night we cross the Fish and
Dragon River, then stagger on
Across the Bird and Rat Hills
Away into the west, asking why
Beacon flares can still be seen,
Worrying lest we be halted
By still more war.

(五)

西使宜天马，由来万匹强。

浮云连阵没，秋草遍山长。

闻说真龙种，仍残老骕骦。

哀鸣思战斗，迥立向苍苍。

Zhang Qian in Han could get
The best horses of the tribesmen
From regions too where the
Good horses were; but today so many
Of the best horses have been killed
In battle, so that on hill pastures
Grasses grow high; now I hear
There is a descendant of
The famous dragon steed, old yet
Vigorous and powerful; seeing
The enemy, he neighs, keen to attack,
Turning his head around to get
The order to advance.

月夜忆舍弟

戍鼓断人行，边秋一雁声。

露从今夜白，月是故乡明。

有弟皆分散，无家问死生。

寄书长不达，况乃未收兵。

THINKING OF MY BROTHERS
ON A MOONLIGHT NIGHT

Drums at the watch-towers beat,
And roads below clear of people;
I think of the frontier as I
Hear the wild geese's autumn cry;
Dew changes to frost, but I feel
Moonlight is not as bright as it was
Back in my old home; now my brothers
Are scattered, and there is no way
For me to know if they are alive
Or dead, for letters cannot come
And the war that keeps us apart
Seems unending.

空　囊

翠柏苦犹食，明霞高可餐。

世人共鲁莽，吾道属艰难！

不爨井晨冻，无衣床夜寒。

囊空恐羞涩，留得一钱看。

THE EMPTY WALLET

Green cedar leaves and gorgeous sun-glow
May be food for the immortals, but not
   for men;
The world is tough and real, my road full
Of hardship; nothing to cook, so leaving
The well stiff with ice; not clothing enough
So sleeping cold through the night; yet
It is bad to have one's wallet completely
Empty, so I leave a coin in it
Just to comfort me.

病　马

乘尔亦已久，天寒关塞深。

尘中老尽力，岁晚病伤心。

毛骨岂殊众，驯良犹至今。

物微意不浅，感动一沉吟。

THE SICK HORSE

For so long have I ridden with you,
Now on the frontier through bitter
Winter; you have worked long and well
And I sadden that you are old and sick;
Only an ordinary horse, they would say,
Yet only I know how fine and loyal
You have been; just an animal, surely!
But to me a noble spirit, worthy of
This song of grief I sing.

发秦州

我衰更懒拙，生事不自谋。

无食问乐土，无衣思南州。

汉源十月交，天气凉如秋。

草木未黄落，况闻山水幽。

栗亭名更嘉，下有良田畴。

充肠多薯蓣，崖蜜亦易求。

密竹复冬笋，清池可方舟。

虽伤旅寓远，庶遂平生游。

此邦俯要冲，实恐人事稠。

LEAVING QINZHOU

As strength declines so do I
Become lazier, more foolish;
Not worrying about food until
Hunger comes; only when cold
Thinking of the south;
Early November in Hanyuan
Is still autumn, with leaves
Still not turned, and lovely
Scenery around; now Chestnut Halt
Is a fine name, the good soil
Of flat lands around growing yams,
Plenty of wild honey to be found,
Thick bamboo groves with many
Shoots, clear water in fishing
Ponds, on which one can boat;
Though too far back for a travelling
Family like ours; to move on there
Surely appeals to me; Qinzhou,
Of course, is an important centre
But I am scared of becoming
Entangled in local affairs which are
Unsuitable for me; local scenery

应接非本性，登临未销忧。

溪谷无异石，塞田始微收。

岂复慰老夫，惘然难久留。

日色隐孤戍，乌啼满城头。

中宵驱车去，饮马寒塘流。

磊落星月高，苍茫云雾浮。

大哉乾坤内，吾道长悠悠。

Is too poor to take my mind from
Our troubles; even in hill valleys
There are no famous sights to see;
Yellow light soil gives poor crops;
In all, a place not good for one
Old already, so I could no longer
Stay; now the redoubt vanishes
Into the dusk as we leave by cart
On through the night; crows caw
From city walls, and we water horses
At pools by the road; above
Is a bright moon and stars
With a thin mist drifting;
How vast the universe! How
Long, how free the road that stretches
Clear out in front of me.

石龛

熊罴咆我东，虎豹号我西。

我后鬼长啸，我前狨又啼。

天寒昏无日，山远道路迷。

驱车石龛下，仲冬见虹霓。

伐竹者谁子？悲歌上云梯。

为官采美箭，五岁供梁齐。

苦云直干尽，无以充提携。

奈何渔阳骑，飒飒惊蒸黎。

AT THE STONE GROTTO

On the east side of us
Comes the grunt of bears,
From the west the roar
Of tigers and leopards;
Spirits of the mountains
Scream behind us, in front
Is the screech of monkeys;
A cold dull day with no ray
Of sun, the way ahead not easy
To pick out; riding up to the Stone Grotto
We see a rainbow in midwinter;
Then wonder who are the bamboo
Cutters whose sad chants rise
As they climb up tall ladders
To meet a five-year order
For arrow shafts to go to Qi and Liang; they
Complaining the supply for straight shafts
Is running out; yet still
Eastern horsemen harry our land.

泥功山

朝行青泥上，暮在青泥中。

泥泞非一时，版筑劳人功。

不畏道途永，乃将汩没同。

白马为铁骊，小儿成老翁。

哀猿透却坠，死鹿力所穷。

寄语北来人，后来莫忽忽。

THE MUD HILLS

Sunrise, and we started to climb
Through the dark mud; sunset and
Still were we in the midst of mud;
Here, the old mud hardly gets a chance
To dry, before the new is made; hard
Work to bridge over the bad places
With planks and stamped dry earth;
One does not mind the everlasting
Journey, but fears falling into
Some hole of mud; my white horse
Has turned as black as iron; my
Little boys look like unsteady old men
As they plug along; monkeys
Are too weighed down with mud to move;
A deer, no strength left, has given up
And died; we ought to send word back
To the north, telling people not to hurry
Through here at this time.

凤凰台

亭亭凤凰台，北对西康州。

西伯今寂寞，凤声亦悠悠。

山峻路绝踪，石林气高浮。

安得万丈梯，为君上上头？

恐有无母雏，饥寒日啾啾。

我能剖心血，饮啄慰孤愁。

心以当竹实，炯然无外求。

PHOENIX SEAT

I have heard there are
Two great rocks they call
The seat of the phoenixes
Lying to the south of Xikangzhou;
They say that in the times
Of Zhou a phoenix came bringing
Glad news of peace; but now
The sound no longer rings
In our ears, so far away it is;
Here mountains are steep,
Roads are not easy to pass,
The rocks are high up in the hills
As though floating on air; how
I wonder, can I get a ladder
And climb up there? Maybe
On top of the Phoenix Seat
Is a motherless bird, each day calling
Miserably, cold and hungry;
I would then be able to take
Out my heart, give my blood
For the phoenix chicks, they taking
The heart instead of the bamboo

血以当醴泉，岂徒比清流。

所重王者瑞，敢辞微命休？

坐看彩翮长，纵意八极周。

自天衔瑞图，飞下十二楼。

图以奉至尊，凤以垂鸿猷。

再光中兴业，一洗苍生忧。

深衷正为此，群盗何淹留？

Berries they cannot find; then this
My final request, that they drink
My blood, for them better than
The best spring water; now the thing
That is important is the happiness
Of the Emperor; my own life is of
No consequence; we know how
The phoenix puts out its great wings
And flies high into the heavens
With wide open eyes seeing all below;
It can take a scroll in its beak
And carry it to the twelfth storey
Of the palace, presenting it
To the greatest Emperor,
Bringing good news of peace
And prosperity for his land;
Now I would that the rule of our court
Again spreads its sway, so that
All bitterness is cleared
From the lives of our people;
In this hope is all my heart!
Robbers, best now get out
Leaving us alone with peace!

乾元中寓居同谷县作歌七首

（一）

有客有客字子美，白头乱发垂过耳。

岁拾橡栗随狙公，天寒日暮山谷里。

中原无书归不得，手脚冻皴皮肉死。

呜呼一歌兮歌已哀，悲风为我从天来！

（二）

长镵长镵白木柄，我生托子以为命！

黄独无苗山雪盛，短衣数挽不掩胫。

SONGS OF A REFUGEE
IN TONGGU

(Seven Poems)

(1)

I, whom they call Du Zimei,
Came to live here awhile; a man,
Grey hair loose about his ears,
Picking up acorns others have overlooked;
Up the bleak sides of hills, that lie so steep
And cold on winter days, I plod;
No news from home back on the Central
   Plains,
So no way to return;
Hands half frozen, skin chapped and numb;
Alas! sad enough is this first song I sing;
Winds come sweeping down the slopes,
Enfolding me in bitterness.

(2)

My spade, my long spade with your white
   wood handle,
By you I live; but these days it is not easy
To find sprouts of yams
On hillsides lying deep in snow;
No matter how hard I tug my garment down

此时与子空归来，男呻女吟四壁静。

呜呼二歌兮歌始放，闾里为我色惆怅。

（三）

有弟有弟在远方，三人各瘦何人强？

生别展转不相见，胡尘暗天道路长。

东飞鴐鹅后鹙鸧，安得送我置汝旁！

呜呼三歌兮歌三发，汝归何处收兄骨？

It will not cover my shivering legs;
Returning home at last, with nothing in my
　hands
But the spade, I find the family
Crying in their misery in a bare room;
Alas! this, my second song, wells to my
　lips,
A song that saddens all the neighbours' hearts.

(3)

Brothers, who are so far away, I know
You must be famished; which of you, I
　wonder,
Is still strong? Life has forced us apart,
And we were borne away without a chance
　of meeting;
Long are the roads which divide us, and
　black with dustof the enemy riders;
I watch the wild geese and cranes fly across;
Would that I could ride with them, and be
　with you!
Alas! this is my third song;
Should I die here, how will you find my
　bones?

（四）

有妹有妹在钟离，良人早殁诸孤痴。

长淮浪高蛟龙怒，十年不见来何时？

扁舟欲往箭满眼，杳杳南国多旌旗。

呜呼四歌兮歌四奏，林猿为我啼清昼！

（五）

四山多风溪水急，寒雨飒飒枯树湿。

黄蒿古城云不开，白狐跳梁黄狐立。

(4)

In Zhongli my little sister lives,
A widow with several pitiful children;
The river Huai is long, its current strong, its dragon
    spirits fierce;
For ten years we have been apart; how may I see
    you now?
Take a boat and sail it to you? Hardly!
For with you too in the distant south
Arrows and banners fly wherever one sets
    eyes;
Alas! this is my fourth song,
Till even by day monkeys in the forest
    weep.

(5)

All round are windy hills; waters rush in
    many streams,
The cold rain beats down, gaunt forest trees
    dripwith moisture;
I look down and see yellow bushes by the
    ancient city,
Clouds lie heavily;
A white fox leaps and a yellow one stands
    stockstill;

我生何为在穷谷？中夜起坐万感集！

呜呼五歌兮歌正长，魂招不来归故乡！

(六)

南有龙兮在山湫，古木岧尦枝相樛。

木叶黄落龙正蛰，蝮蛇东来水上游。

我行怪此安敢出，拔剑欲斩且复休。

呜呼六歌兮歌思迟，溪壑为我回春姿！

And I ponder just why my life should be
Wasted in this lonely valley;
At night I rise up, plagued with troubles;
Alas! this is my fifth song, a long one,
    surely!
You may call my spirit and it will not come:
It has returned to my old village home.

(6)

To the south there lies a dragon in its pool;
Old trees rise high into the sky,
Their branches entwined;
Yellow leaves turn and fall, the dragon lies
    dormant;
From the east come poisonous snakes: I
    wonder howthey dare!
I would draw a sword, yet cannot strike;
Alas! this, my sixth song, lingers on the
    air;
The day is warm, and spring once more
Seems to have returned to streams and
    valleys.

(七)

男儿生不成名身已老，三年饥走荒山道。

长安卿相多少年，富贵应须致身早。

山中儒生旧相识，但话宿昔伤怀抱。

呜呼七歌兮悄终曲，仰视皇天白日速！

So here am I: a man who has grown old
And gained no fame; in these three years of
  famine
While I have been tramping wild hill paths,
In the capital the great officials are still
  young;
One must expect young men to strive
For wealth and position;
Back in the mountains the scholars, old
  friends of mine,
Talk sadly of old times, hiding the scars of
  their struggles;
Alas! now my seventh song ends quietly;
I raise my eyes, and see how quickly the
  sun goes down.

成都府

翳翳桑榆日，照我征衣裳。

我行山川异，忽在天一方。

但逢新人民，未卜见故乡。

大江东流去，游子日月长。

曾城填华屋，季冬树木苍。

喧然名都会，吹箫间笙簧。

信美无与适，侧身望川梁。

鸟雀夜各归，中原杳茫茫。

初月出不高，众星尚争光。

自古有羁旅，我何苦哀伤！

CHENGDU

Sunset makes even my travel clothing
A little brighter; I have covered
Many roads and now arrive in a new
World for me; meeting new people,
Unable to say if ever I shall see
My old home again; now the great river
Flows east, never halting, as indeed
My days of wandering have been;
A walled city enclosing fine houses;
Trees green though winter days;
A great centre full of the sound
Of people and their music; yet even
The excitement of all this does not
Take away my loneliness, so I turn
And look back at the road, its bridges
And streams; birds are returning to
Their nests; the Central Plains are far away,
How can I ever return to them?
Tonight the moon is low, so that
Stars compete with their light;
Always there have been travellers,
Why should I lament?

又于韦处乞大邑瓷碗

大邑烧瓷轻且坚，

扣如哀玉锦城传。

君家白盌胜霜雪，

急送茅斋也可怜。

ON ASKING FOR A BOWL
OF PORCELAIN

Dayi porcelain, so light and hard!
At Chengdu they say it sounds
With the wistful note of jade
When tapped; in your home one sees
Dishes of it outshining frost and snow
In purity; to have some come now
To my poor hut would be having thought
For my poor condition.

蜀　相

丞相祠堂何处寻，锦官城外柏森森。

映阶碧草自春色，隔叶黄鹂空好音。

三顾频烦天下计，两朝开济老臣心。

出师未捷身先死，长使英雄泪满襟。

THE TEMPLE OF ZHUGE LIANG

Looking for the temple
To Zhuge Liang I find it
Outside the city under
Cypresses; green grasses
Amongst the paving stones
Reminding of spring, little birds
Hidden amongst the branches all
A-twittering; and I think of how
Three times the prince called
Zhuge Liang to serve him, how then
Two reigns gave this statesman
Room to plan; sad that he had
To die before he gained victory,
Leaving great men of
Succeeding generations
To grieve for him.

堂　成

背郭堂成荫白茅，缘江路熟俯青郊。

桤林碍日吟风叶，笼竹和烟滴露梢。

暂止飞乌将数子，频来语燕定新巢。

旁人错比扬雄宅，懒惰无心作解嘲。

HOME BUILT

My cottage outside the city
Is built at last with thatched roof
By the bend of a river where
A well used path runs out
To the fields; forest trees
Give shade from the sun; winds
Rustling through their leaves; giant
Bamboo that grows so tall sways
In the mists, dew dripping
Down its branches; crows come
And go, the old with their chicks!
Swallows flit in seeking a place
To nest; friends come and say
It is like the home of Yang Xiong,
But I do not feel like
Arguing with them all.

狂　夫

万里桥西一草堂，百花潭水即沧浪。

风含翠筱娟娟净，雨浥红蕖冉冉香。

厚禄故人书断绝，恒饥稚子色凄凉。

欲填沟壑惟疏放，自笑狂夫老更狂。

THE CRAZY FELLOW

My thatched hut west
Of the Wanli Bridge
Near the Baihua waters;
A pleasant retreat
With green bamboos beside
Bending like shy girls
When kissed by the wind;
Fragrance from pink lotus flowers
After the rain; but still
Rich frineds have sent me no help
And the faces of my children
Are pale with hunger; when crazy
One becomes even gay
Before dying in some hole; so
Laughing at one's old age
And craziness, the crazier
Does one become.

江　村

清江一曲抱村流，长夏江村事事幽。

自去自来堂上燕，相亲相近水中鸥。

老妻画纸为棋局，稚子敲针作钓钩。

但有故人供禄米，微躯此外更何求？

THE RIVER BY OUR VILLAGE

Clear waters wind
Around our village,
With long summer days
Full of loveliness;
Fluttering in and out
From the house beams
The swallows play;
Waterfowl disport together
As everlasting lovers;
My wife draws out
A chessboard on paper
While our little boys
Bend needles into fish hooks;
Herbs are what a sick man needs,
What more could I wish for?

野　老

野老篱边江岸回，柴门不正逐江开。

渔人网集澄潭下，估客船随返照来。

长路关心悲剑阁，片云何意傍琴台？

王师未报收东郡，城阙秋生画角哀。

OLD MAN IN THE COUNTRY

A fence of woven bamboo winding
Along the river bank;
A picket gate set askew
Yet true to the bending
Stream; fishermen setting
Their nets in clear waters;
Cargo boats sliding quietly
Behind the rays of the setting sun;
I think back on the bitterness
Of the long road down from Jiange,
Idly puzzle why a piece of cloud
Drifts around a distant tower, then
Wonder why no report comes from the army
On the recovery of our eastern lands;
Look across to the towers on the city wall
With autumn colours beside and the sound of
Bugles and their touch of melancholy.

题壁上韦偃画马歌

韦侯别我有所适，知我怜君画无敌。

戏拈秃笔扫骅骝，欻见麒麟出东壁。

一匹龁草一匹嘶，坐看千里当霜蹄。

时危安得真致此，与人同生亦同死！

WRITTTEN ON A WALL BESIDE
THE HORSES PAINTED
BY WEI YAN

My friend Wei comes
In farewell, and knowing
How I love his art,
Picks up my old brush
And in fun starts to paint;
Soon marvellous horses
Show up on my eastern wall,
Here one grazing, there
Another neighing; the kind
Of horses for long distances;
Would now that these could
Come to life and serve one
Through life and death.

南　邻

锦里先生乌角巾，园收芋栗不全贫。

惯看宾客儿童喜，得食阶除鸟雀驯。

秋水才深四五尺，野航恰受两三人。

白沙翠竹江村暮，相送柴门月色新。

OUR SOUTHERN NEIGHBOUR

Our village celebrity, in his smart cap
— A black, cornered one — has
A fine garden, and cannot be said
To be poor; his children, it would
Seem, have been trained to welcome
Visitors with smiles; always enough
Food about for even the birds
To flock there; the water in autumn
Is quite shallow, and the little
Farm boat we go in will take but three
Of us; the white beach and green
Bamboos fade out in the dusk, after
We have said our farewells at
The garden gate, under the faint light
Of a new moon.

恨　别

洛城一别四千里，胡骑长驱五六年。

草木变衰行剑外，兵戈阻绝老江边。

思家步月清宵立，忆弟看云白日眠。

闻道河阳近乘胜，司徒急为破幽燕！

THE UNHAPPY FAREWELL

Leaving Luoyang I have
Gone over four thousand *li*
Of roads in these five
Or six years; now finding
Grasses and woods once more
Withering as I roam outside
Jiange; ever growing older
While living beside this river;
Last night I thought of my home
As I paced under the moonlight,
Today I lie on my bed;
Watching clouds drift,
Thinking of my brother;
I hear that at Heyang
There has been a victory
And I wonder if our commander
Can break through to the
Plains of You and Yan.

后　游

寺忆曾游处，桥怜再渡时。

江山如有待，花柳更无私。

野润烟光薄，沙暄日色迟。

客愁全为减，舍此复何之？

TRAVELLING AGAIN

I remember the temple and bridge
Passed before, hills and streams
That all seem to have lain
In waiting for me; flowers
And willows so warmly opening out,
Their beauty in welcome; out on
The plains, smoke showed thin;
The last rays of sunlight lingered
On warm sands; then a traveller's
Worries ceased, for nowhere could
A better halting place be found.

春夜喜雨

好雨知时节，当春乃发生。

随风潜入夜，润物细无声。

野径云俱黑，江船火独明。

晓看红湿处，花重锦官城。

GOOD RAIN ON A SPRING NIGHT

A good rain falling
Just when it should
In springtime; riding
On the wind it fills
A whole night, soaking
The land with its goodness;
Clouds hang heavily over
Country paths; a lone light
Shines from a passing boat;
Morning and I see a damp
Redness on the branches,
Laden down with flowers.

春水生二绝(选一)

(一)

二月六夜春水生，

门前小滩浑欲平。

鸬鹚鸂鶒莫漫喜，

吾与汝曹俱眼明。

SPRING FLOOD

(One of Two Poems)

(1)

On the sixth of the second month
At night, a spring flood came;
Morning and in front of my door
I saw how water had about covered
The sandy beach there; you
Cormorants and you ducks, do not
Splash so happily! Don't
You see as clearly as I
The dangers in front of you?

江上值水如海势，聊短述

为人性僻耽佳句，语不惊人死不休！

老去诗篇浑漫与，春来花鸟莫深愁。

新添水槛供垂钓，故著浮槎替入舟。

焉得思如陶谢手，令渠述作与同游！

RIVER WATERS THAT ARE
LIKE THE SEA

I am not quite as other men,
Being simply fond of writing good lines;
Deciding that unless I can
Compose really excellent
Ones, I will go on trying
Right up to death; in all
These years I just give away
My poems to any who will
Take them; when spring comes
And there are flowers and birds
I am not too depressed, for
Beside the river I have set
A railing to lean over as I fish;
I make a raft to do instead
Of a boat, and ever hope to write
Poetry like Tao Yuanming or
Xie Lingyun, so that as I wander
I can enjoy its cadence.

水槛遣心二首（选一）

（一）

去郭轩楹敞，无村眺望赊。

澄江平少岸，幽树晚多花。

细雨鱼儿出，微风燕子斜。

城中十万户，此地两三家。

LEANING OVER THE RAILING
I FREE MY HEART

(One of Two Poems)

(1)

My home in the suburbs,
Commanding a fine view
Unobstructed by any village
So that I can see
Far into the distance
With but a quiet stream beside
Low banks, and a view of a tree
In blossom at sunset; able to watch
Small fish rise in the rain
And swallows that clip the breeze
As they fly; in the city are
A hundred thousand households;
Here, but two or three.

江畔独步寻花七绝句 (选二)

(六)

黄四娘家花满蹊，千朵万朵压枝低。

留连戏蝶时时舞，自在娇莺恰恰啼。

(七)

不是爱花即欲死，只恐花尽老相催。

繁枝容易纷纷落，嫩蕊商量细细开。

ALONG THE RIVERSIDE, ALONE
AND LOOKING AT THE FLOWERS

(Two of Seven Poems)

(6)

In the garden of Lady
Huang the Fourth, flowers fill
The whole place; blossom
Weighs the branches low;
Gay butterflies flit in
And around, accompanied by
The joyous song of birds.

(7)

Not that I love flowers
More than life; simply
Scared that when they
Have faded, I will grow
Old much faster; petals
Scatter too easily;
Better if buds were made
To open up more gradually.

进　艇

南京久客耕南亩，北望伤神坐北窗。

昼引老妻乘小艇，晴看稚子浴清江。

俱飞蛱蝶元相逐，并蒂芙蓉本自双。

茗饮蔗浆携所有，瓷罂无谢玉为缸。

OUT ON THE BOAT

To Chengdu, the southern capital,
Has come an old man, tuned
Farmer, who still feels bitter
When he sits and stares northwards;
Now finding forgetfulness when
He paddles with his wife in a little boat,
Watching their children bathing
In clear waters; and the butterflies
Courting each other; seeing two
Lotus blossoms on one stalk together;
Taking with them tea
Or else sugar-cane juice,
Thinking how for drinking
Ordinary pottery is as good
As the finest jade.

茅屋为秋风所破歌

八月秋高风怒号，卷我屋上三重茅。

茅飞渡江洒江郊，

高者挂胃长林梢，下者飘转沉塘坳。

南村群童欺我老无力，

忍能对面为盗贼，公然抱茅入竹去。

唇焦口燥呼不得，归来倚杖自叹息。

俄顷风定云墨色，秋天漠漠向昏黑。

布衾多年冷似铁，娇儿恶卧踏里裂。

SONG OF THE AUTUMN WIND
AND THE STRAW HUT

An autumn wind ripped clear
Three layers of thatch from my hut
Spreading it over the river,
Along the banks, into the marsh
Or driving it up into branches
Of tall trees.

Over from the south village ran
A bunch of boys, seeing me old
And feeble, stealing the thatch
In front of my eyes; hauling it
Off to their bamboo grove, I
Shouting at them until my mouth
Was dry, throat sore; then
Going inside with a sigh, leaning
On my stick; the gale stopped
But black clouds gathered
Hastening the night.

I looked at my bedding quilt, now
As cold as iron, all torn with
The restless feet of my children;

床头屋漏无干处，雨脚如麻未断绝。

自经丧乱少睡眠，长夜沾湿何由彻？

安得广厦千万间，大庇天下寒士俱欢颜，

风雨不动安如山！

呜呼！何时眼前突兀见此屋？

吾庐独破受冻死亦足！

Rain streamed through the roof
Like unbroken strings of hemp
Drenching all, and I pondered on
How much sleep I had lost since
This rebellion began, hoping
The night would pass swiftly,
Wondering in my dream whether
It would be possible to build
An immense house with thousands
Of rooms, where all who needed
Could take welcome shelter; a mansion
As solid as a hill, not fearing
Wind or rain; then thinking how
If only such could be,
Would I be content to see my poor hut
Demolished with I myself
Frozen to death.

百忧集行

忆年十五心尚孩，健如黄犊走复来。

庭前八月梨枣熟，一日上树能千回。

即今倏忽已五十，坐卧只多少行立。

强将笑语供主人，悲见生涯百忧集。

入门依旧四壁空，老妻睹我颜色同。

痴儿不知父子礼，叫怒索饭啼门东。

BALLAD OF THE
HUNDRED SORROWS

Rising fifteen and just a child
Of nature, running around like
A little brown calf; in late summer
When pears and dates were ripe,
Climbing the trees each day so many times;
And now, so suddenly it seems, I come
Towards fifty; sitting and resting
More than getting up and going out;
Always trying to put on a pleasant face
When I visit my superior, yet ever my mind
Tormented with a host of worries;
Going back home, seeing the place as bare
As ever; my wife looking at my troubled face
And guessing my inner thoughts
While the children not even bothering
To give the politeness due a father,
Simply fussing and shouting at being unable
To find food in the kitchen.

不　见

不见李生久，佯狂真可哀。

世人皆欲杀，吾意独怜才。

敏捷诗千首，飘零酒一杯。

匡山读书处，头白好归来。

NOT SEEN

A whole lifetime seems
To have passed since
Last I saw Li Bai; a pity
He had to pretend to be
Crazy, but there were
Men of affairs who wished
To kill him; now it seems
I alone have pity for
That brilliance which
Shows up so vividly in his
Thousand poems; battered
By storms he has but
The solace of wine; in
His retreat at the Kuang Hills
He studied; can he, with hair
Growing white, but return there?

花　鸭

花鸭无泥滓，阶前每缓行。

羽毛知独立，黑白太分明。

不觉群心妒，休牵俗眼惊。

稻粱沾汝在，作意莫先鸣。

THE COLOURED DUCK

The coloured duck
So clean and shining
Comes up to the front
Of the steps;
Other ducks seeing it
Standing alone, as
Different from them
As black is from white;
Not troubling
What others think of it;
Surely,
Hardly wise to bring
Such attention to itself;
Better for it quietly
To take its share of what
There is, never
Being heard first.

少年行

马上谁家白面郎，

临阶下马坐人床。

不通姓氏粗豪甚，

指点银瓶索酒尝。

TOO YOUNG

Who is, I wonder mildly,
This little pretty
Whipper-snapper; jumping
From his horse
So cockily, sitting down
Uninvited; too sure
Of himself to say
Who he is; haughtily
Pointing to the silver
Jug, demanding I pour
Wine for him?

遭田父泥饮，美严中丞

步屧随春风，村村自花柳。

田翁逼社日，邀我尝春酒。

酒酣夸新尹，畜眼未见有！

回头指大男："渠是弓弩手。

名在飞骑籍，长番岁时久。

前日放营农，辛苦救衰朽。

差科死则已，誓不举家走！

今年大作社，拾遗能住否?"

A FARMER, IN PRAISE OF THEGOVERNOR, INVITES ME TO DRINK

Strolling out to enjoy the spring,
Seeing in every village willows
Bursting into green, flowers blooming,
Then meeting a farmer friend, inviting
Me at the festival to taste the new wine he
    has brewed;
As he drinks, he praises the new governor
The best he has ever known; turning then
And showing me his eldest son, trained
Archer in the cavalry scouts, who
Ordinarily could not hope for discharge —
Now sent home to help because
His father is sick and old; now, the family
Feels they would do anything for this
Governor; even should it mean death,
Said they, would they support him to
The end;

"Now, "said he, "we'll celebrate
The spring holiday properly; stay
With us, Your Honour, while I tell

叫妇开大瓶，盆中为吾取。

感此气扬扬，须知风化首。

语多虽杂乱，说尹终在口。

朝来偶然出，自卯将及酉。

久客惜人情，如何拒邻叟？

高声索果栗，欲起时被肘。

指挥过无礼，未觉村野丑。

月出遮我留，仍嗔问升斗。

The wife to bring a whole great
Jar of wine!"Then handing me
A big bowl for drinking;
Grateful to find
Such friendly feelings around,
Do I understand how important
The good official is; my
Farmer friend is voluble,
Bringing in the governor
To his every story; strange,
It was early morning when I
Came out to walk, and so soon
Has it become late afternoon; still
A newcomer needs friendliness,
So will not want to repel it when
It comes to him; my host shouts
For more to eat; I get up to go,
He pushes me down, village fashion,
Not really rude; then when
The moon has risen, he still
Invites me to stay on, insisting
That I drink more.

大麦行

大麦干枯小麦黄，妇女行泣夫走藏。

东至集壁西梁洋，问谁腰镰胡与羌！

岂无蜀兵三千人？部领辛苦江山长！

安得如鸟有羽翅，托身白云还故乡！

SONG OF THE BARLEY

The barley is overripe, wheat
Now turns yellow; wives weep
For husbands gone to hide;
From Ji and Bi in the east
Over to Liang and Yang in the west,
Tribesmen Hu and Qiang are
Everywhere robbing crops; ask why
The three thousand Sichuanese soldiers
Do not help more, all we can say
Is that commands come, but the area
To be covered is too great; now for me
The only way I might return would be
To take the wings of a bird, then
Entering a cloud, fly home.

闻官军收河南河北

剑外忽传收蓟北，初闻涕泪满衣裳。

却看妻子愁何在，漫卷诗书喜欲狂！

白日放歌须纵酒，青春作伴好还乡。

即从巴峡穿巫峡，便下襄阳向洛阳。

GOOD NEWS OF THE RECOVERY
OF THE CENTRAL PLAINS

News of the recovery of our lost lands
Reaches down to us in Sichuan; crying
With happiness, my tears fall on my clothes;
I turn to see my wife and children;
Excitedly, I start to roll up my papers,
Half crazy with the good news; though
The sun has not set, I feel I must drink
And sing; perhaps together with the
Spring shall we come back home again;
Down through the Yangzi Gorges shall
We sweep, then on to Xiangyang, finally
Arriving in old Luoyang.

舟前小鹅儿

鹅儿黄似酒，对酒爱新鹅。

引颈嗔船逼，无行乱眼多。

翅开遭宿雨，力小困沧波。

客散层城暮，狐狸奈若何？

THE GOSLINGS IN FRONT
OF MY BOAT

Yellow goslings with a colour
As rich as one good wine
Held up against another;
You so lovable making me
Feel wine is already before
Me; you stick out your heads
And fiercely try to halt
My boat; confusing me
With your playfulness; spreading
Your wet wings, but they
Are not strong enough yet
For you to use! When those
Who play here go back to city
Homes and a fox comes,
What then will you do?

将赴成都草堂途中有作先寄
严郑公五首(选一)

(四)

常苦沙崩损药栏，也从江槛落风湍。

新松恨不高千尺，恶竹应须斩万竿！

生理只凭黄阁老，衰颜欲付紫金丹。

三年奔走空皮骨，信有人间行路难。

RETURNING TO THE
THATCHED HUT IN CHENGDU
AND PRESENTING TO
DUKE OF ZHENG

(One of Five Poems)

(4)

At times the stop bank will collapse
And my plots of medicinal plants
Be washed away by the running waters;
I would that young pines I have
Planted were already tall, but
The many bamboos that shoot up around
Choke them; even for the basic
Things of livelihood, we depend
On you of exalted rank! Now to
Relieve my sadness will you just
Give me the pill of immortality?
These three yaers have I put out
My strength in vain, learning only
How bitter the roads can be.

草　堂

昔我去草堂，蛮夷塞成都。

今我归草堂，成都适无虞。

请陈初乱时，反复乃须臾。

大将赴朝廷，群小起异图。

中宵斩白马，盟歃气已粗。

西取邛南兵，北断剑阁隅。

布衣数十人，亦拥专城居。

其势不两大，始闻蕃汉殊。

西卒却倒戈，贼臣互相诛。

焉知肘腋祸，自及枭獍徒。

THE THATCHED HUT

I moved out of my thatched hut
When the tribesmen drove into
Chengdu; today I have come
Home again as peace returns;
The attack was sudden and not
Prepared for; our commander had
Gone to court, and foolish
Young officers conspired, killing
A white horse at midnight,
Taking mad oaths with its blood;
Sending some west to take over
Forces there, others north to
Break the wooden track through
The pass at Jiange; some stupid
Persons took important positions
In this city or that, and then
Started to fight each other, giving
The tribesmen a lead in; in
The west, the soldiers rose,
Everywhere there was killing,
The internal struggle causing
Self-destruction; decent folk
Were all indignant, there being

义士皆痛愤，纪纲乱相逾。

一国实三公，万人欲为鱼。

唱和作威福，孰肯辨无辜？

眼前列杻械，背后吹笙竽。

谈笑行杀戮，溅血满长衢。

到今用钺地，风雨闻号呼。

鬼妾与鬼马，色悲充尔娱。

国家法令在，此又足惊吁！

贱子且奔走，三年望东吴。

弧矢暗江海，难为游五湖。

不忍竟舍此，复来薙榛芜。

入门四松在，步屧万竹疏。

旧犬喜我归，低徊入衣裾。

No longer any law; so many leaders,
So much suffering among the people;
Some tried to make things worse
All the time; none cared for justice;
They tortured, they revelled,
Playing and laughing as the blood
Of the innocent ran down the gutters
Outside; screams and groans can still
Be heard in bad weather; women
And horses of the dead became
Property of the murderers, surprising
For government and law still exist;
Then all I could do was to go
And for three years I gazed out
Towards the east, but there
Were troubles also and I
Could not make up my mind to go
On to the Five Lakes; now as I
Love this place I have come back
To clear away the brambles; coming in,
I am happy to see my four pines
Still live; in my grass sandals I go
Through the bamboos, meeting
My old dog so glad to see me
That he gets up under my gown;

邻里喜我归，沽酒携胡芦。

大官喜我来，遣骑问所须。

城郭喜我来，宾客隘村墟。

天下尚未宁，健儿胜腐儒。

飘飘风尘际，何地置老夫！

于时见疣赘，骨髓幸未枯。

饮啄愧残生，食薇不敢余。

Neighbours are happy I have
Come back, carrying much wine
To me; then Governor Yan too
Sent a man to see what I needed
And all around was welcome; yet
I know there is no real peace
As yet; strong soldiers are today
More useful than old scholars;
Yet perhaps because of all this chaos
There is no place for one like me;
Though useless still I have a little life left;
Whatever good now comes to me
I will appreciate and be content.

四　松

四松初移时，大抵三尺强。

别来忽三载，离立如人长。

会看根不拔，莫计枝凋伤。

幽色幸秀发，疏柯亦昂藏。

所插小藩篱，本亦有堤防。

终然枨拨损，得愧千叶黄？

敢为故林主，黎庶犹未康！

避贼今始归，春草满空堂。

THE FOUR PINES

When first transplanted
My four pines were more
Than three feet high; now
Three years later, they
Are as tall as I; with
Care I look around them,
Seeing that roots are firm
Though branches have been
Battered a little; good
They still shine a deep
Bright green; though thin,
Their spreading
Arms extend; I once put up
A picket fence to guard them,
But the fence is broken
And the needles have paled;
Yet how dare I assert ownership,
Seeing peace has not yet come
To our land; and again,
Escaping rebel clutches, I return
To see spring grasses around
My empty home; look over

览物叹衰谢，及兹慰凄凉。

清风为我起，洒面若微霜。

足为送老资，聊待偓盖张。

我生无根蒂，配尔亦茫茫。

有情且赋诗，事迹可两忘。

勿矜千载后，惨澹蟠穹苍！

The few possessions left, and see
How much is ruined; yet
To be able to come back has made
Me happy; a soft breeze
Caresses and soothes with its cool,
Keeping me young; pines, I would
You grow tall, spread out, give
Shade; I, a man without roots,
Without ties, am your friend;
Moved I sing some poems; things
That now take place
And their results, will soon
Drop into the past; no use
For me to talk of a thousand
Years ahead; yet ever, my pines,
You will rise up majestically
Into the heavens.

登　楼

花近高楼伤客心，万方多难此登临！
锦江春色来天地，玉垒浮云变古今。
北极朝廷终不改，西山寇盗莫相侵。
可怜后主还祠庙，日暮聊为梁甫吟。

ON GOING UP A TOWER

Somehow even the flowers blooming
So gaily around the tower
Make me feel sad, for everywhere
Today is trouble; spring colours by
The Jin River are a gift from heaven;
Flying clouds over the Jade Mountains
Are like the changes of history;
Now in the north, imperial rule
Is at last steady; already it is useless
For invaders from the west to attack;
I sigh at the temple to the Second Emperor,
And as sunset comes chant
A song of Zhuge Liang.

绝句四首（选一）

（三）

两个黄鹂鸣翠柳，

一行白鹭上青天。

窗含西岭千秋雪，

门泊东吴万里船。

SHORT IMPRESSIONS

(One of Four Poems)

(3)

From vivid green willows
Comes the call of two orioles;
A file of white water birds
Rises into the clear blue heavens; as if
Held in the mouth of my window
Are the mountain ranges with
Their snows of many autumns;
Anchored by our gate are
The long distance boats of Wu.

忆昔二首(选一)

(二)

忆昔开元全盛日，小邑犹藏万家室。

稻米流脂粟米白，公私仓廪俱丰实。

九州道路无豺虎，远行不劳吉日出。

齐纨鲁缟车班班，男耕女桑不相失。

宫中圣人奏云门，天下朋友皆胶漆。

THINKING OF OTHER DAYS

(One of Two Poems)

(2)

In those prosperous times
Of the period of Kai Yuan,
Even a small county city
Would be crowded with the rich;
Rice flowed like oil and both
Public and private granaries
Were stuffed with grain; all
Through the nine provinces
There were no robbers on
The roads; travelling from home
Needless to pick an auspicious
Day to start; everywhere carriages
With folk wearing silk or brocade;
Farmers ploughed, women picked
Mulberries, nothing that did
Not run smoothly; in court
Was a good Emperor for whom
The finest music was played;
Friends were honest with each other

百余年间未灾变，叔孙礼乐萧何律。

岂闻一绢直万钱，有田种谷今流血。

洛阳宫殿烧焚尽，宗庙新除狐兔穴。

伤心不忍问耆旧，复恐初从乱离说。

小臣鲁钝无所能，朝廷记识蒙禄秩。

周宣中兴望我皇，洒血江汉身衰疾。

And for long there had been
No kind of disaster; great days with
Rites and songs, the best of other times,
Laws the most just; who could
Have dreamed that later a bolt
Of silk would cost ten thousand
Cash? Now the fields farmers
Tilled have become covered
With bloodshed; palaces at Luoyang
Are burnt, and temples to
The imperial ancestors are full
Of foxes and rabbit burrows!
Now I am too sad to ask
Questions of the old people,
Fearing to hear tales
Of horror and strife;
I am not able, but yet
The Emperor has given me
A post, I hoping that he
Can make the country
Rise again like King Xuan
Of Zhou; though for myself
I simply grieve that now age
And sickness take their toll.

宿　府

清秋幕府井梧寒，独宿江城蜡炬残。

永夜角声悲自语，中天月色好谁看？

风尘荏苒音书绝，关塞萧条行路难。

已忍伶俜十年事，强移栖息一枝安。

AUTUMN NIGHT

Autumn night in headquarters, and I
With a stark *wutong* tree for company
Have come to rest; the candle gutters
And I cannot sleep; a bugle sounds,
Reminding me of the never ending war;
The moonlight is full of beauty, but
Only I am awake to see it, and to weep
Over the lack of news from home;
Perpetual fighting, so who would know when
Roads will be open again? Ten years
Of a refugee's life, and now here
In this old building, a moment's peace.

春日江村五首（选一）

（一）

农务村村急，春流岸岸深。

乾坤万里眼，时序百年心。

茅屋还堪赋，桃源自可寻。

艰难昧生理，飘泊到如今。

SPRING IN THE VILLAGE ON
THE RIVER BANK

(One of Five Poems)

(1)

Farmers busy in every village;
Waters flowing deep in every stream;
All over the world things
Are the same, each spring
One has the same feelings;
My cottage of thatch is still
Worth singing a song about;
Surely the Utopia of Tao Yuanming
Can be found; not knowing how
To make a livelihood I have
Been wandering all these years.

旅夜书怀

细草微风岸，危樯独夜舟。

星垂平野阔，月涌大江流。

名岂文章著，官应老病休！

飘飘何所似，天地一沙鸥。

NIGHT THOUGHTS OF
A TRAVELLER

Thin reeds, and from the land
A soft breeze; our mast stands
Tall and stark in the night
And I am alone; stars hang
Over the great plain, and
The moon moves with the flowing river;
Fame may not come together
With literary merit;
A broken-down, worn-out
Official should simply rest!
It seems I am but as a sand bird
Blown before the elements.

移居夔州作

伏枕云安县，迁居白帝城。

春知催柳别，江与放船清。

家事闻人说，山光见鸟情。

禹功饶断石，且就土微平。

MOVING HOUSE TO KUIZHOU

From my sick-bed in Yun-an
I now move to Kuizhou;
Green willows chase out
The spring, as our boat
Goes swiftly downstream;
I listen to folk talking
About their farm work,
Feeling close to the birds
That soar over the hills;
I am grateful to Yu the Great
For leaving some level spots
When he cut the mountains through.

引 水

月峡瞿塘云作顶，乱石峥嵘俗无井。

云安沽水奴仆悲，鱼复移居心力省。

白帝城西万竹蟠，接筒引水喉不干。

人生流滞生理难，斗水何直百忧宽。

LEADING WATER DOWN

A mongst the clouds that lie
Over the river gorges, there
Are masses of rock, but no wells;
In Yun-an servants complained
That cash had to be paid for water;
Now here, much can be saved, as
By the White Emperor City are endless groves
Of giant bamboo, which are cut,
Made into piping to bring
Water down; for strangers as wo are
In a different land, ever there are
Difficulties; water seems
But a small thing, yet simply
Having it clear worries away.

负薪行

夔州处女发半华，四十五十无夫家。

更遭丧乱嫁不售，一生抱恨长咨嗟。

土风坐男使女立，应当门户女出入。

十犹八九负薪归，卖薪得钱应供给。

SONG OF THE
FIREWOOD VENDORS

With hair
Already changing colour,
Middle-aged yet
Still unmarried, are
The working women of
This Kuizhou; for
With wars raging,
They have no chance
For husbands; so
Live lives full
Of resentment and despair;
Here, in this place
Old customs persist,
Women on their feet
Out working, while
Men sit watching
Their homes; here
Most women climb hills
Seeking firewood, carrying
It down on their backs
To sell for food;

至老双鬟只垂颈，野花山叶银钗并。

筋力登危集市门，死生射利兼盐井。

面妆首饰杂啼痕，地褊衣寒困石根。

若道巫山女粗丑，何得此有昭君村？

Even in old age
They wear hair
In girlish plaits;
Sticking wild flowers
And pretty leaves into it
With silver hairpins;
Over the mountains
They climb, packing for
The market great loads
On their backs;
Or else seek work at
Salt wells, risking
Lives to earn what they may;
With faces from which
Nothing may erase
Marks of bitterness
And tears; their days
They pass in barren lands,
Little clothing
To keep out the cold, cut
Off from life; some say
They are ugly, yet
Not far from here
Is a village, famous birthplace
Of that beauty of beauties,
Wang Zhaojun.

最能行

峡中丈夫绝轻死，少在公门多在水。

富豪有钱驾大舸，贫穷取给行舴艋子。

小儿学问止《论语》，大儿结束随商旅。

欹帆侧舵入波涛，撇漩捎濆无险阻。

朝女白帝暮江陵，顷来目击信有征。

SONG OF THE ABLEST MEN

People on Sichuan rivers
Do not fear death; few in
Official mansions, many out
In boats, the rich and powerful
With big ones, the poor in small;
Many children are taught
Only the *Confucian Analects*
And when they grow older
They become traders, setting
Out in boats that must ride
The waves through gorges,
Ignoring the many dangers
Of whirlpools and rapids; in
The morning setting out
From Baidi, then at evening
Getting down to Jiangling;
This I have seen myself
So I know well it is true;

瞿塘漫天虎须怒，归州长年行最能。

此乡之人气量窄，误竞南风疏北客。

若道士无英俊才，何得山有屈原宅。

Waters at Qutang rise
To the sky, and those at Huxu
Dash madly on rocks; but yet our
Guizhou boatmen are so able they can
Navigate through all hazards;
One trouble here is that folk
Are narrow-minded, liking only
Those of their locality, but not
We who come from the north; yet
Should you say they are not able,
Then I ask did not Qu Yuan
Come from a mountain home near here?

白 帝

白帝城中云出门，白帝城下雨翻盆。

高江急峡雷霆斗，古木苍藤日月昏。

戎马不如归马逸，千家今有百家存。

哀哀寡妇诛求尽，恸哭秋原何处村？

WHITE EMPEROR CITY

Cloud coming out of
The city gate, heavy rain
Pouring outside the city wall; a torrent
Of water dashing madly
Through the gorges, waves
Struggling against each other
With a sound like thunder;
Trees and vines shut out the light;
Horses which have galloped
To war are not so happy as those
Left at home; of a thousand
Families, but a hundred remain;
Widows in endless sorrow moaning
Over a desolate autumn plain,
And I wonder which of the villages
They have come from.

古柏行

孔明庙前有老柏，柯如青铜根如石。

霜皮溜雨四十围，黛色参天二千尺。

君臣已与时际会，树木犹为人爱惜。

云来气接巫峡长，月出寒通雪山白。

忆昨路绕锦亭东，先主武侯同闷宫。

崔嵬枝干郊原古，窈窕丹青户牖空。

落落盘据虽得地，冥冥孤高多烈风。

THE ANCIENT CYPRESS

Fronting the temple to Zhuge Liang
An ancient cypress, branches like
Bronze, roots as strong as stone,
Its bark so bright that water
Simply slips off, a massive bole
Its tip reaching up into the clouds
That drift away down the gorges;
A chill moon rises and all
Is white as a snowy mountain;
Liu Bei and Zhuge Liang, Emperor
And counsellor brought strength as they
Worked, together, and the land prospered
So that folk still remember them and love
This tree; recently I passed
The Jin pavilion in Chengdu,
Seeing a shrine to Zhuge Liang
In one court of the temple of Liu Bei;
But the painted rooms were
Silent and empty; outside
Trees still stood in their place
But being so tall their branches
Must take the force of great winds;

扶持自是神明力，正直元因造化工。

大厦如倾要梁栋，万牛回首丘山重。

不露文章世已惊，未辞剪伐谁能送？

苦心岂免容蝼蚁，香叶终经宿鸾凤。

志士幽人莫怨嗟，古来材大难为用。

An ancient cypress held erect
By its spirit, so straight, so regular
In form, the power of heaven manifested
Through it; a big house about to collapse
Needs a strong buttress and each succeeding
Year shows how important this becomes;
Even when young, Zhuge Liang was seen
   to be
Brilliant; when he took office it was but he
Who could hold away the enemy,
Using his ability to save the land;

An ancient cypress with such great
   branches,
Perhaps now ants eat out your bitter
   heart-yet maybe
You once gave home to a phoenix! Men who
Are determined or who would become
   hermits
Do not hate, do not sigh! Here stands
A glorious tree yet from old till now none
Has been able to use it.

宿江边阁（选一）

螟色延山径，高斋次水门。

薄云岩际宿，孤月浪中翻。

鹳鹤追飞静，豺狼得食喧。

不眠忧战伐，无力正乾坤！

NIGHT IN THE
PAVILION BY THE RIVER

Evening haze creeps up hill paths,
I lie in the pavilion overlooking
The river; light clouds envelop
Cliff sides, and the moon's reflection
Is twisted by the waters;
Cranes and storks rest after
Their flight; wild beasts howl
As they seek their prey; sleep
Does not come to me, for still
I worry about war, knowing I have
No way to set the world aright.

咏怀古迹五首(选一)

(三)

群山万壑赴荆门，生长明妃尚有村。

一去紫台连朔漠，独留青冢向黄昏。

画图省识春风面，环佩空归月夜魂。

千载琵琶作胡语，分明怨恨曲中论。

THOUGHTS ON ANCIENT PLACES

(One of Five Poems)

(3)

Ranges of mountains, then
So many valleys running down
To Jingmen; the village home of
The Bright Concubine still stands;
Going from the imperial palace
She croossed wide deserts; now
Her lonely grave faces the dust of
A frontier sunset; and I think
Of her face full of the colours of spring
Seen in many paintings, and dream of her
Jade ornaments tinkling as her ghost
Returns; now for long years, wild music
From tribesmen's guitars has sounded
Her bitterness and hate
Echoing in every line of their song.

壮　游

往昔十四五，出游翰墨场。

斯文崔魏徒，以我似班扬。

七龄思即壮，开口咏凤凰。

九龄书大字，有作成一囊。

性豪业嗜酒，嫉恶怀刚肠。

脱略小时辈，结交皆老苍。

饮酣视八极，俗物多茫茫。

东下姑苏台，已具浮海航。

到今有遗恨，不得穷扶桑。

王谢风流远，阖庐丘墓荒。

TRAVEL IN THE MIDDLE YEARS

When around fourteen or fifteen
I started to enter literary circles;
Some of the masters compared me
With Ban Gu and Yang Xiong of old;
From seven onward, indeed, were
My thoughts turned to old heroes;
The first poem I wrote was on
The phoenix; nine, and I could
Practise writing big characters,
Already having composed much;
Unconventional and fond of wine,
Strong-willed and hating wicked ones;
No longer playing with silly
Companions, but seeking out the old
And experienced so that we could
Take in the universe together,
Cutting free of the commonplace;
Finishing my visit to Gusu
In the east I meant to sail on
Over the sea; still sorry that I
Did not go to Isles of the Sacred Tree;
   in Gusu
Glories of the past were forgotten,
The royal tombs overgrown, though

剑池石壁仄，长洲荷芰香。

嵯峨阊门北，清庙映回塘。

每趋吴太伯，抚事泪浪浪。

蒸鱼闻匕首，除道哂要章。

枕戈忆勾践，渡浙想秦皇。

越女天下白，鉴湖五月凉。

剡溪蕴秀异，欲罢不能忘。

归帆拂天姥，中岁贡旧乡。

气劘屈贾垒，目短曹刘墙。

忤下考功第，独辞京尹堂。

The Sword Lake stood beside
A crumbling wall; lotus in the ponds
Was still fragrant; north of Chang Men
Was the big memorial temple
To Wu Taibo; paying my respects
I mourned for him as a patriot, then
Thought of the man with his dagger
In the belly of a fish, of Zhu Maichen
Whose seal surprised the petty official,
And again of Gou Jian who slept
On a pile of firewood, then
How the First Emperor of Qin
Crossed the river; the girls
Of Yue were the loveliest, and too
There was a lake cool even in
Midsummer; Shanxi, and one saw
Glorious scenery; experiencing
So much I could not get it all
Out of my mind, nor do I still;
Returning to the north by boat
I visited Tianmu Mountain;
Back at home again, now in
The prime of life, I was recommended
For an official post, and
Fearing no competition, wen on
To Chang'an; there I did not get on
With ministers, and failed to gain
The office I sought, so after saying
Farewell, returned home once more,

放荡齐赵间，裘马颇清狂。

春歌丛台上，冬猎青丘旁。

呼鹰皂枥林，逐兽云雪冈。

射飞曾纵鞚，引臂落鹙鸧。

苏侯据鞍喜，忽如携葛强。

快意八九年，西归到咸阳。

许与必词伯，赏游实贤王。

曳裾置醴地，奏赋入明光。

天子废食召，群公会轩裳。

脱身无所爱，痛饮信行藏。

黑貂宁免敝，斑鬓兀称觞。

Going off for pleasure, riding
A horse to Qi and Zhao, wearing furs,
Leading a full and free life;
Spring and I sang songs in
Famous places, spending winter
Hunting around Qingqiu, whistling
For falcons from amongst the trees,
Joining the chase over Yunxue
Hills; shooting arrows as I galloped,
Each arrow bringing down its brid!
My companion Su Yu rejoiced from
His saddle, thinking he was hunting
With Ge Qiang the ancient general;
And so for eight years did this
Pleasant kind of life go on, until
I returned to the capital, and began
To make friends with poets, and too
One of the princes, so was invited
To many happy feasts, feeling
Quite at home with him; then I wrote
Poems for the court, and the Emperor
Summoned me at once, I meeting officials
Who looked so proud that I went away
Not wanting to be like them; at that time
What pleased me was drinking and doing
Exactly as I wished, never caring,
Feeling that even if I wore a
Sable robe, it would soon be worn out
And I would spend declining years
Drinking wherever I could;

杜曲换耆旧，四郊多白杨。

坐深乡党敬，日觉死生忙。

朱门务倾夺，赤族迭罹殃。

国马竭粟豆，官鸡输稻粱。

举隅见烦费，引古惜兴亡。

河朔风尘起，岷山行幸长。

两宫各警跸，万里遥相望。

崆峒杀气黑，少海旌旗黄。

禹功亦命子，涿鹿亲戎行。

翠华拥吴岳，螭虎啖豺狼。

In my old home village of Duqu, poplars
And ash trees grew thickly on graveyards;
So many elders had died that I became
   an elder
Myself; each day I was concerned
With birthdays, funerals, and livelihood
In general, with the respect of all;
This was the tim when the powerful
Conniving behind their great red doors
Would kill and steal, but then they
And their families would in turn
Be slaughtered; army horse exhausted
All fodder available, yet officials
Demanded rice and millet to feed fighting
Cocks; I tell of this to show
What the people suffered from the
   government;
There are many examples in history
To show how a dynasty rises, then falls;
Throughout the north, the air was dark
With battle; the Emperor fled south
And two courts flew imperial standards,
Yet each so distant from the other; the war
Raged on in both east and west,
While, like Yu the Great,
The old Emperor handed rule to his son
Who kept on fighting the rebels,
Directing all from his capital
At Fengxiang, here our armies
Were trained to be as tigers

爪牙一不中，胡兵更陆梁。

大军载草草，凋瘵满膏肓。

备员窃补衮，忧愤心飞扬。

上感九庙焚，下悯万民疮。

斯时伏青蒲，廷诤守御床。

君辱敢爱死，赫怒幸无伤。

圣哲体仁恕，宇县复小康。

哭庙灰烬中，鼻酸朝未央。

小臣议论绝，老病客殊方。

郁郁苦不展，羽翮困低昂。

To wolves, but the first offensive
Was turned to defeat, so that
The tribesmen became even more
Fierce; then again imperial armies
Suffered reverse and one felt
Pity for the imperial ancestors
And the common people in their
Sufferings; at this time I became
A censor to the throne, and did
My duty in putting forward
Advice persistently, saying
To him that if in any way
The Emperor was humiliated, then
The minister should die; then just
Imperial anger sought punishment
But other ministers intervened
And my life was saved; as time
Went on, and peace gradually established,
The court returned to Chang'an,
And worshipped before the ashes
Of imperial temples, weeping as they
Gathered in the palace hall;
My description however is only that
Of a small official, who has said
All he wants to say, who now away
From court, is old, sick and a stranger
In a far off place, sad because he
Has been able to do so little, and now
Like a bird flies aimlessly; winds

秋风动哀壑，碧蕙捐微芳。

之推避赏从，渔父濯沧浪。

荣华敌勋业，岁暮有严霜。

吾观鸱夷子，才格出寻常。

群凶逆未定，侧伫英俊翔。

Of autumn sound up the valleys,
The scent of the orchid fades away;
Jie Zhitui wanted no reward for
Going to exile with his master, and
The fisherman of Qu Yuan was happy
Sailing on his river; great exploits
Are like flowers that come and go;
Plants with the most beautiful leaves
Are cut down quickest; now we do
Have a great statesman, the best of
Our time; the wicked have not yet
Been brought to justice, so one like
Him has still much yet to do.

秋兴八首

(一)

玉露凋伤枫树林，巫山巫峡气萧森。

江间波浪兼天涌，塞上风云接地阴。

丛菊两开他日泪，孤舟一系故园心。

寒衣处处催刀尺，白帝城高急暮砧。

(二)

夔府孤城落日斜，每依北斗望京华。

AUTUMN FEELINGS

(Eight Poems)

(1)

Dew-drops like jade seem
To cut the maple trees;
By the Wu Gorge and among
Mountains beside, a dismal
Breath soughs through forests;
Waves of the river seem to rise
Up into the sky, dark clouds
Drive in; now as I see
Chrysanthemums old sorrows
Revive; my hopes for
A return home seem bound up
In this boat lying at anchorage;
Now all around people are
Getting winter clothing ready,
And by White Emperor City
Rises the sound of washing mallets
Beating clothes to cleanness.

(2)

Sunset over the lonely city
Of Kuizhou passes; I face
The Great Bear looking
Towards the capital; as in

听猿实下三声泪，奉使虚随八月槎。

画省香炉违伏枕，山楼粉堞隐悲笳。

请看石上藤萝月，已映洲前芦荻花。

（三）

千家山郭静朝晖，日日江楼坐翠微。

信宿渔人还泛泛，清秋燕子故飞飞。

匡衡抗疏功名薄，刘向传经心事违。

同学少年多不贱，五陵衣马自轻肥。

Old tales, my tears accompany
The cries of monkeys, though
Unlike legend I am unable to
Float home down the Milky Way;
White walls and incense burners
In ministers' halls I cannot see
From my bed; only from the battlements
Opposite my mountain home comes
The melancholy sound of bugles!
Look! the moonlight which
Shone on ivy-covered stones
Now glints from the tassels
Of reeds by the river bank.

(3)

A mountain city of but
A thousand families;
Under the light of dawn
I sit as each day I have sat
Watching the hills in blue
From this room above the river;
Seeing fishermen returning
After their work at night,
Looking at swallows still
Flitting here and there;
Then thinking of how I lost
My post as censor, how I have
Failed to become a great scholar,
And so on to old fellow students,
Of how they will be riding,
Splendidly clad on stout horses
Around Chang'an.

（四）

闻道长安似弈棋，百年世事不胜悲。

王侯第宅皆新主，文武衣冠异昔时。

直北关山金鼓振，征西车马羽书驰。

鱼龙寂寞秋江冷，故国平居有所思。

（五）

蓬莱宫阙对南山，承露金茎霄汉间。

西望瑶池降王母，东来紫气满函关。

云移雉尾开宫扇，日绕龙鳞识圣颜。

4

They say Chang'an is like
A chessboard, though for these
Past years games played there
Have had the sadness of defeat;
New tenants occupy palaces
Of princes and nobles; neither
Civil nor military officials
Are as those before; straight
Through the northern passes
Comes the clash of gongs, the beat
Of war drums; straight west are
Horses, chariots and dispatch riders;
Here where fish and dragon lie
Quietly in the cool autumn waters,
I can live in peace and ponder
Over old times gone by.

5

Penglai Palace faces
The south mountains; there
Golden columns placed
To catch the dew stand proudly;
Looking west one thinks of
The Jade Lake of the Queen
Of the Western Heavens; then east
And thinks of Lao Zi riding
Through the purple mist of the Pass;
Like clouds opening,
Pheasant tail fans move apart
And the face of the Emperor

一卧沧江惊岁晚，几回青琐点朝班。

瞿塘峡口曲江头，万里风烟接素秋。

花萼夹城通御气，芙蓉小苑入边愁。

珠帘绣柱围黄鹄，锦缆牙樯起白鸥。

回首可怜歌舞地，秦中自古帝王州。

昆明池水汉时功，武帝旌旗在眼中。

Can be seen above his robe
Of shining dragon scales; now
I sleep a little by this quiet river,
Awake and realize how late it is!
Feeling sad that so few times
I have attended court audiences.

(6)

The Qutang Gorge is separated
From the Winding River at Chang'an
By so many miles of wind and mist,
Yet both share this autumn; the court
Went on procession from the pavilion
Of flowers down the imperial way
To the park, eagerly awaiting couriers
Bringing news from the frontier;
Yellow cranes, carved columns,
Screens inlaid with pearls, and then
White birds that sported around
Pleasure boats with masts as white
As ivory, and ropes of coloured silk;
Sadly one thinks back on the palace
Where song and dance reigned; a capital
For long lines of rulers throughout
Our past.

(7)

Kunming Lake is a reminder
Of the glory of Han, and one
Conjures up the vision of
Fluttering standards of the
Emperor Wu; there too stands

织女机丝虚夜月，石鲸鳞甲动秋风。

波漂菰米沉云黑，露冷莲房坠粉红。

关塞极天惟鸟道，江湖满地一渔翁。

（八）

昆吾御宿自逶迤，紫阁峰阴入渼陂。

香稻啄余鹦鹉粒，碧梧栖老凤凰枝。

佳人拾翠春相问，仙侣同舟晚更移。

彩笔昔曾干气象，白头吟望苦低垂。

The image of the Weaving Maid
Alone in the moonlight, while
The stone whale beside seems
To move in the autumn wind;
Now here with me, I see wild rice
Floating on the waves, think
Of the dark clouds passing, seeing
How chilly dew strips
Red petals from lotus blooms,
And how but birds can take the path
Through steep gorge cliffs,
Feeling that I am but an old fisherman set amongst
The vastness of rivers and lakes.

(8)

A long winding road led past
Kunwu and Yusu, where reflections
Of the Purple Peak
Lit up the Meipi Lake; parrots
Have left a few grains on stalks
Of grain fed to them, and here
Stands the *wutong* tree where once
A phoenix perched;
Lovely ladies picked up coloured
Feathers, handing them out as
Spring presents; along with
Immortals one could sail in a boat
Late in the evening; once
With a gay pen I wrote of it all,
But now white head bent low, I have
Little strength to write of it again.

孤　雁

孤雁不饮啄，飞鸣声念群。

谁怜一片影，相失万重云。

望尽似犹见，哀多如更闻。

野鸦无意绪，鸣噪亦纷纷。

THE LONE WILD GOOSE

Too sad to drink or eat
The lone wild goose broods,
Giving a mournful cry
In his search for the flock
Now lost in distant cloud;
It strains its eyes looking
Into the distance, thinking
It can see the others,
Replying to cries that are but
Echoes of its own; the sound
Waking other birds from
Their sleep, confusing them
With its sadness.

日　暮

牛羊下来久，各已闭柴门。

风月自清夜，江山非故园。

石泉流暗壁，草露滴秋根。

头白灯明里，何须花烬繁。

SUNSET

Sheep and cattle have long
Come down from the hills;
Stock gates in every home
Are closed; a pleasant night
With a breeze and moon; yet
It is borne on me that these
Hills and streams are not
Really my home; down in the gullies
Rapids swish over the rocks;
Dew lies on the grass of the plains;
My hair is grey already, why
Does the candle throw off sparks?

登　高

风急天高猿啸哀，渚清沙白鸟飞迴。

无边落木萧萧下，不尽长江滚滚来。

万里悲秋常作客，百年多病独登台。

艰难苦恨繁霜鬓，潦倒新停浊酒杯。

WRITTEN ON AN
AUTUMN HOLIDAY

These days of autumn, the clouds
Are high; wind rises in strength;
Far away the cry of monkeys can
Be heard, giving people a sorrowful
Feeling; skimming the white sands
And the water, waterfowl fly; falling
Leaves rustle as they come through
The air; the Yangzi seems endless
With its waters rolling on incessantly;
So many autumns have I now spent
Away from home, with sickness for
A companion; now do I climb high
Above the river by myself,
Troubles and sorrow have turned my hair
Grey; sick and poor, I now
Even stop drinking wine!

暂往白帝复还东屯

复作归田去，犹残获稻功。

筑场怜穴蚁，拾穗许村童。

落杵光辉白，除芒子粒红。

加餐可扶老，仓廪慰飘蓬。

ON GETTING BACK TO
THE FARM AT DONGTUN,
AFTER A TRIP TO THE
WHITE EMPEROR CITY

Back at my farm I see
Harvest still unfinished;
In stamping down a threshing-floor
No ants should be crushed, then
In bringing in sheaves, enough
Gleanings should be left for
Village boys to gather; husking rice
Makes pounding pestles shine white,
Leaving us grain tinged red;
To eat more may help an old man
And a good harvest stored encourages
A mere traveller like me.

又呈吴郎

堂前扑枣任西邻，无食无儿一妇人。

不为困穷宁有此，只缘恐惧转须亲。

即防远客虽多事，便插疏篱却甚真。

已诉征求贫到骨，正思戎马泪沾巾。

ON ASKING MR. WU FOR THE
SECOND TIME

Do please let your neighbour
Who lives to the west of you
Pick up the dates in front of
Your home; for she is a woman
Without food or children; only
Her condition brings her to
This necessity; surely she
Ought not to fear you, because
You are not a local man, yet
It would be good of you to try
And help her, and save her
Feelings; so do not fence off
Your fruit; heavy taxation is
The cause of her misery; the
Effect of war on the helpless
Brings us unending sorrow.

观公孙大娘弟子舞剑器行
并序

　　大历二年十月十九日，夔州别驾元持宅，见临颍李十二娘舞剑器，壮其蔚跂。问其所师，曰："余公孙大娘弟子也。"开元三载，余尚童稚，记于郾城观公孙氏舞剑器浑脱，浏漓顿挫，独出冠时。自高头宜春梨园二伎坊内人，洎外供奉舞女，晓是舞者，圣文神武皇帝初，公孙一人而已！玉貌锦衣，况余白首！今兹弟子，亦匪盛颜。既辨其由来，知波澜莫二。抚事慷慨，聊为《剑器行》。昔者吴人张旭善草书书帖，数尝于邺县见公孙大娘舞西河剑器，自此草书长进，豪荡感激，即公孙可知矣！

322

ON SEEING THE SWORD
DANCE OF A PUPIL
OF MADAME GONGSUN

In the second year of the Da Li period, the tenth month, the nineteenth day, at the home of Yuan Chi, magistrate of Kuizhou, I saw the girl Li the Twelfth from Linying do a sword dance. She was so good that I asked her who was her teacher, and she told me that she was taught by Gongsun the First, who I saw in the third year of Kai Yuan do both the Sword Dance and the Felt Cap Dance at Yancheng. Gongsun did her dance with strength and freedom. In the beginning of Xuan Zong's period, Gongsun was the best of the two schools — Pear Garden and Spring Court. Her beauty faded as my white bairs grew, and now even her student does not look young. I saw how the movements of teacher and pupil were the same. This thing I have seen has caused me to write a poem. Once Zhang Xu of Wu, a calligrapher, saw Gongsun doing the West River Sword Dance at Ye, and afterwards his writing improved vastly, showing both strength and rbythm.

昔有佳人公孙氏，一舞剑器动四方。

观者如山色沮丧，天地为之久低昂。

㸌如羿射九日落，矫如群帝骖龙翔。

来如雷霆收震怒，罢如江海凝清光。

绛唇珠袖两寂寞，晚有弟子传芬芳。

临颍美人在白帝，妙舞此曲神扬扬。

与余问答既有以，感时抚事增惋伤。

先帝侍女八千人，公孙剑器初第一。

五十年间似反掌，风尘澒洞昏王室。

Once there was a beauty called
Gongsun whose Sword Dance
Was loved by all; row on row
The audience looked spellbound at her,
Feeling as they were seeing heaven
Struggling against the earth;
She bent back and it seemed
There came the suns shot out by Yi;
When she rose in the air it was
As if there were gods astride
Dragons in the clouds; watching her
One could see thunder, lightning,
Storm, then quiet rays over
A peaceful sea; but soon her
Loveliness was heard of no more;
Now her art is carried on but
By this beauty of Linying in far
Kuizhou, where she dances and sings;
Talking with her I think of
Other days, and am filled with sadness;
In the old court were eight
Thousand ladies, and of them Gongsun
Led in the Sword Dance;
This fifty years have passed
Like the turning of a hand
And the old court has been
Submerged under the waves of war;

梨园弟子散如烟，女乐余姿映寒日。

金粟堆南木已拱，瞿唐石城草萧瑟。

玳筵急管曲复终，乐极哀来月东出。

老夫不知其所往，足茧荒山转愁疾。

Pear Garden dancers have vanished
Like the mist, and now but
The beauty of this one shines
In the chill sunlight; trees
By the imperial graves have
Grown high; grasses in this old city
By the Qutang Gorge have faded;
Feasting, music and song have ended;
After-pleasure comes the sadness
Of watching the moon in the east;
Just an old man like me, not knowing
Where he goes, but simply pushing
Unwilling legs up lonely hills.

写怀二首(选一)

(一)

劳生共乾坤，何处异风俗？

冉冉自趋竞，行行见羁束。

无贵贱不悲，无富贫亦足。

万古一骸骨，邻家递歌哭。

鄙夫到巫峡，三岁如转烛。

全命甘留滞，忘情任荣辱。

THOUGHTS

(One of Two Poems)

(1)

Work comes into the lives of all,
Can anywhere custom change this?
Men pursue fame and wealth
But lose their freedom in the race;
If power were not
Grabbed by some, others would
Not be so sad; if there were
No great rich, the poor would be
More satisfied with what they have;
Death is the fate of all; here
One laughs — there another weeps;
Now these three years
Here in the Yangzi Gorges, my life
Has been like a flickering flame
In the wind; I stay to regain
Some health; already old I take news
Both good and bad with a smile;

朝班及暮齿，日给还脱粟。

编蓬石城东，采药山北谷。

用心霜雪间，不必条蔓绿。

非关故安排，曾是顺幽独。

达士如弦直，小人似钩曲。

曲直吾不知，负暄候樵牧。

Once an official, now in my old age,
Eating coarse rice each day, living
In my thatched cottage east of the city;
Going out to search for
Medicinal herbs in northern gullies,
Paying attention only to roots
Under frost and snow, avoiding the growth
Above; yet this has just been my peculiar
Way of doing things
Without any particular purpose;
A really great man is like a straight
    bowstring,
A small one like a crooked hook;
Who straight, who crooked, is the problem
I ponder over as I warm my back
Under the sun, waiting to meet
Buffalo boys and woodcutters as they come
    along.

短歌行赠王郎司直

王郎酒酣拔剑斫地歌莫哀！

我能拔尔抑塞磊落之奇才。

豫章翻风白日动，鲸鱼跋浪沧溟开。

且脱佩剑休徘徊！

西得诸侯棹锦水，欲向何门趿珠履？

仲宣楼头春色深，青眼高歌望吾子。

眼中之人吾老矣！

A LITTLE SONG FOR WANG, THE YOUNG OFFICIAL

Wang, my young friend, you who sit
Drinking your wine,
Jabbing your sword into the ground
And sining so sadly; surely
I understand your thwarted ability,
How you stand so well against
Winds and sun like a tree,
Or as a whale cutting through
The waves; come now, leave
That sword alone and rest a while!
As you go west and come to
The seats of the great, so will you
Be rowing around waterways,
Wondering which of them you will ask
For patronage! Here this springtime
On the Wang Can tower, I sing you
This song, happy to be looking at you,
Expecting great things of you, for
I know well I have become
An old man already.

登岳阳楼

昔闻洞庭水，今上岳阳楼。

吴楚东南坼，乾坤日夜浮。

亲朋无一字，老病有孤舟。

戎马关山北，凭轩涕泗流。

ON YUEYANG TOWER

For long I have heard of
This Dongting Lake, but
This the first time I
Climb the Yueyang Tower;
Seeing how southeast
The lands of Chu break from those
Of Wu, with our earth as if
Floating on night and day;
Neither home folk nor friends
Have sent me any message; sick
And old I can travel but by boat;
Over far mountains, away
To the north, still there is war
And I lean over the railings,
Full of sadness.

岁晏行

岁云幕矣多北风，潇湘洞庭白雪中。

渔父天寒网罟冻，莫徭射雁鸣桑弓。

去年米贵缺军食，今年米贱大伤农。

高马达官厌酒肉，此辈杼柚茅茨空。

楚人重鱼不重鸟，汝休枉杀南飞鸿。

况闻处处鬻男女，割慈忍爱还租庸。

THOUGHTS BEFORE NEW YEAR

The year draws in, and around
Dongting Lake high winds drive
Down snow, nets freezing in
The hands of fishermen, so that
They leave fishing to shoot
Wild geese with arrows made
Of mulberry branches; last year
Grain was dear and the army
Scantily provided;
Now the price has dropped
And the peasants suffer; haughty
Offcials prance on gallant steeds
After feasting to their fill, while
In the homes of the poor there is
No money to buy yarn for weaving;
Folk here enjoy eating fish,
So it is bettes to let
Wild geese fly on in peace; now too
I hear boys and girls are being sold
By families, who loving them yet
Are forced to meet tax payments

往日用钱捉私铸，今许铅锡和青铜。

刻泥为之最易得，好恶不合长相蒙！

万国城头吹画角，此曲哀怨何时终？

In this way; once the government
Forbade counterfeiting;
Now in private mints
Lead and tin are added to copper;
Simpler to use just clay for coinage
And not try to fool the people! Now
From every city wall comes the blare
Of bugles; when will these sad times pass?

清明二首（选一）

（二）

此身飘泊苦西东，右臂偏枯半耳聋。

寂寂系舟双下泪，悠悠伏枕左书空。

十年蹴鞠将雏远，万里秋千习俗同。

旅雁上云归紫塞，家人钻火用青枫。

AT THE TIME OF QING MING

(One of Two Poems)

(2)

Tossed here and there,
At times west, then east;
Right arm paralysed,
Half deaf, lying in
This anchored boat,
Tears falling to my pillow;
Writing characters in the air
With my left hand; for years
I have wandered with my children,
Kicked around like a ball,
Or as if I was being tossed
On a swing as is the custom here;
I see wild geese
Fly back through clouds
To the frontier; people here
Still make fire by boring
In a wooden hole, using maple
Sticks for this; towers of Qin

秦城楼阁烟花里，汉主山河锦绣中。

春去春来洞庭阔，白蘋愁杀白头翁。

Have pavilions bright
With flowers, the hills of Han
Are embroidered with colour;
With spring the waters rise
And the Dongting Lake becomes broad;
I am like some pale waterweed,
Knowing troubles will soon cause the end
Of this grey-headed old man.

江　汉

江汉思归客，乾坤一腐儒。

片云天共远，永夜月同孤。

落日心犹壮，秋风病欲苏。

古来存老马，不必取长途。

RIVER BANK

Here sits a man by
The river bank, who thinks
To return home; he is an
Ordinary scholar, drifting
Like a piece of cloud above;
At night, I am lonely
As the moon, but at sunset
I am still of good heart;
In these autumn winds
My illness gets better;
In past times, they were kind
To old horses, not sending
Them off on tiring journeys
After they had served so long.

客 · 从

客从南溟来，遗我泉客珠。

珠中有隐字，欲辨不成书。

缄之箧笥久，以俟公家须。

开视化为血，哀今征敛无！

TRAVELLER'S GIFT

From the south came a friend
Leaving me with pearls
That were as if made of tears;
In them seemed to be something
Written, but I could not read
It; then I put them away
In a box, waiting the day
For tax-collectors to come, but
When I opened it I found that
Pearls had turned to blood,
And felt how bad it was,
There were no tear-gems left
To fill their demands.

蚕谷行

天下郡国向万城，无有一城无甲兵！

焉得铸甲作农器，一寸荒田牛得耕？

牛尽耕，蚕亦成。

不劳烈士泪滂沱，男谷女丝行复歌。

SONG OF THE SILKWORMS
AND GRAIN

Everywhere in all
Our ten thousand towns
Rises the clash of weapons;
Better now were all these
Hammered into farm tools
So that lands gone to waste
Could be tilled again;
Lads busy with oxen,
Lasses with silkworms;
No longer the need for soldiers
To weep such pools of tears;
Men growing grain, women
Spinning silk; so together
Songs would rise from
The people's lips again.

江南逢李龟年

岐王宅里寻常见，

崔九堂前几度闻。

正是江南好风景，

落花时节又逢君。

MEETING LI GUINIAN
IN JIANGNAN

Often you went to the palace
Of Prince Qi, and then you
Sang again and again for Cui Di;
Jiangnan scenery is now at
Its best; as blossom falls,
So do we meet again!